John A Garciá

2

F. Chris Garcia
Rudolph O. de la Garza

The University of New Mexico
The Colorado College

The Chicano

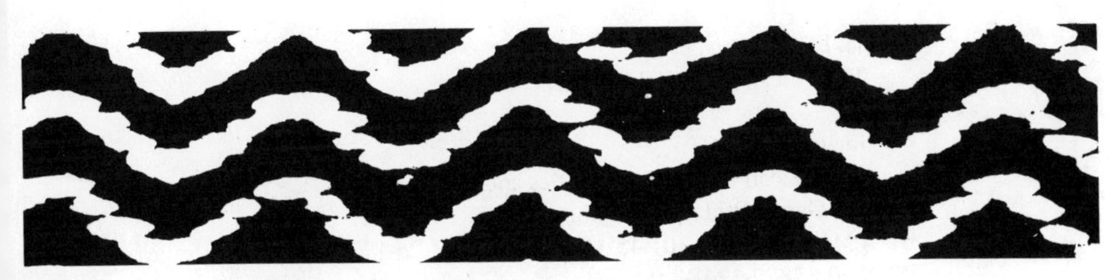

Political Experience

Three Perspectives

Duxbury Press

North Scituate, Massachusetts

Library of Congress Cataloging in Publication Data

Gracia, F Chris.
The Chicano political experience.

Includes index.
1. Mexican Americans–Politics and suffrage.
I. De la Garza, Rudolph O., joint author. II. Title.
E184.M5G359 301.45'16'872073 76-17716
ISBN 0-87872-124-X

Duxbury Press
A Division of Wadsworth Publishing Company, Inc.

The Chicano Political Experience: Three Perspectives was edited and prepared for composition by Bea Gormley. Interior design was provided by Dorothy Thompson and the cover was designed by Nancy Gardner.

L.C. Cat. Card No.: 76-17716
ISBN 0-87872-124-X
Printed in the United States of America
1 2 3 4 5 6 7 8 9 – 80 79 78 77

This book is dedicated to:

La Raza—The Chicano People;

Sandra, Elaine, and Tanya Garcia,
wife and daughters;

Jo-Ann de la Garza and Frank Jesus Cajas,
sister and brother

Contents

CHAPTER NINE
Chicano Political Leadership: "El que a dos amos sirve, con uno queda mal."
144

CHAPTER TEN
Political Change Strategies: "Con deseos no se hacen templos."
161

CHAPTER ELEVEN
Analysis, Conclusions, and Prospects
189

Preface

During the third quarter of this century, this nation has witnessed dramatic changes in the political behavior of nonwhite minority groups. Changes in the political life of the Chicano are particularly significant because as Americans of Mexican/Spanish ancestry they have been involved in the politics of the United States since 1848, and yet most of their fellow citizens are ignorant about the essence of the Chicano political experience. This ignorance and lack of concern persists today despite increased media coverage of Chicano activities; in fact, it might well be argued that the media has not significantly contributed to public awareness but has instead generated confusion and exacerbated long-standing antagonisms. It is our hope that this book will help correct these problems.

Our effort may best be described as a descriptive-analytical text. The majority of the book consists of description—of contemporary Chicano culture, of Chicano political history, of the various elements that constitute the Chicano political movement. We have also attempted to explain why Chicanos remain politically weak by analyzing the Chicano experience according to competing theories of the distribution of power in contemporary America. The models we use to assess Chicano politics are (1) the open, competitive pluralist model, (2) the closed, undemocratic elitist model, (3) a relatively new variation of the elitist approach, the internal colonialism model. Throughout the book we examine various aspects of the Chicano political experience according to the tenets of each of these approaches.

We have made every effort to incorporate every available piece of research on Chicano politics into this text. Although it is unlikely that we achieved our objective, we are confident that this is the most comprehensive coverage of this subject currently available. We therefore hope and expect that our work will generate debate and prompt others to expand and improve on our efforts. Given, furthermore, that it is virtually impossible to include in any text the most current data, we have made every effort to insure that our study provides the interested reader with a means for interpreting new political events.

We have also done our utmost to be objective and have relied on empirical studies whenever possible. This is not, however, a value-free book. As Chicanos, we strongly feel that Americans of Mexican/ Spanish ancestry have fared poorly at the hands of the American political and economic system, especially considering the contributions we have made to this nation. We also believe that the economic and political institutions of the United States are suffering from major structural problems, and that many of these problems are particularly damaging to Chicanos and other nonwhite minorities. There can be no doubt, in our judgment, that Chicanos have too long been deprived of the basic American promises of life, liberty, and the pursuit of happiness, and that for too many years they have been denied the civil rights and liberties that are the birthright of every citizen but which only the priviliged few truly enjoy.

We are indebted to all the scholars, journalists, poets, activists, and students whose writings and conversations provided us with so much material.

Our special thanks go to Professors Ralph Guzman, Rudolph Gomez, Carlos Cortés, Biliana Cisin-Sain, Adalijiza Sosa Riddell, Ray Sandoval, and Charles Cotrell for their comments and criticisms on earlier versions of the manuscript. We would also like to thank Mrs. Helen Lynch for her assistance in preparing the manuscript, and Beatrice Gormley for the attention and skill with which she edited our work.

This book is certain to be criticized by Chicanos and non-Chicanos of all political persuasions. Since ours was a truly joint and cooperative effort, we will take refuge from these attacks by officially declaring that each of us has the right to blame the other for any mistakes, but we each reserve the right to take credit for whatever might be praiseworthy.

Models of the Political Process:

Implications for Chicano Politics

Sometime in the mid-1960s a previously little-heeded but important force began to push its way into America's political consciousness. Although Americans of Mexican and Spanish ancestry are among the most senior of United States ethnic groups, they had remained relatively unknown and unappreciated as a significant social, economic, or political segment of our society. However, the boycotts, walk-outs, strikes, marches, pickets, and other dramatic manifestations signaled other Americans that a unique and revitalizing element—the Chicano movement—had entered full-force into the political processes of the United States.

The Chicano movement is seeking fundamental changes in American society—changes in the distribution of wealth and power and in the basic norms, attitudes, and institutional arrangements. In order for Chicanos to use those strategies and tactics which are most likely to succeed, they must take into consideration the present distribution of power in the United States. There is, however, considerable disagreement on the essential nature of American politics, or how power *is* actually distributed.

Social scientists have constructed several models that attempt to describe how power and influence are distributed in our society and how the American political process operates. We will examine three of these models: (1) pluralistic democracy, (2) elitism, and (3) internal colonialism. The pluralist and elitist models are the two major opposing interpretations of the United States political process. Actually these are general categories of various models devised by political scientists. For example, the elitist models include the "power elite" models as well as others in which a small and distinctive part of the population is in a position of control.[1] The internal colonial model was developed in the mid-1960s to describe the special situation of racial minorities in the United States.[2] Each of these models will be described and evaluated throughout this book in terms of how much each contributes to our understanding of the Chicano political experience.

The Pluralist Model

The dominant model used by students of politics to explain the distribution of power in this society is the *pluralist* model. This model has been used both to describe and analyze how power is distributed in this country and to suggest how it should be allocated.[3]

Characteristics of Pluralist Model

Although the specific details may vary from observer to observer, there are several features which are of central importance to any pluralist model.[4]

Multiple centers of power. The key element is that the policy-making process rests on a base of multiple centers of power, none of which is entirely sovereign. Power is widely dispersed both formally and informally, and these power centers are relatively free of control by any higher ultimate ruler. This is a group model in that the competing actors in the political arena are primarily groups—organizations, associations, and other forms of collective interests.

These groups, which are assumed to be relatively equal in resources and influence, compete with one another to exert influence on the decision makers of our society; that is, our public authorities. Out of this relatively open competition among groups, which involves a complicated process of bargaining and negotiation, comes public policy. The resources that enable groups to compete are several, and no one group commands a majority of all resources. Thus a great variety of groups form and compete for power. The principal resources are money, legitimacy, and commitment of members.

Multiple access points. Another characteristic of the pluralist system is that there are many points along the decision-making route at which groups seeking to influence the system can exert their pressure. No legitimate group is permanently excluded from access to the decision-making process. For example, even though Afro-Americans (blacks) had been largely excluded from exerting influence in the executive or legislative branch, they did have an organization, the NAACP (National Association for the Advancement of Colored People), that was successful in presenting their case before the courts in the 1940s and 1950s.

Gradual change. The policy process in a pluralistic system is of necessity an incremental one, one which progresses little by little. This is a logical consequence of the features previously mentioned, such as the wide dispersal of power and the processes of bargaining and negotiation. Change is gradual, it is consistent with early policy, and most importantly it in no way fundamentally alters the basic distribution of social, economic, or political power in society. In a pluralistic system, therefore, comprehensive, fundamental change is unlikely.

Nonpolitical issues. Two other features of the pluralist model are important for the ultimate success or failure of Chicano politics. First, many issues lie outside the boundaries of the political process. These issues—for example, problems in the private sector of the economy such as unemployment—are considered out of control by the legal authority of government. Pluralists may consider the results of past discriminatory practices unfortunate, but not as subject to direct solution through political processes.

Semipublic decision making. Second, many important public questions are placed in the hands of semipublic decision-making bodies, beyond the reach of such popular means of control as elections. The most important of these semipublic bodies is the bureaucracy. Administrative bodies are increasingly an integral part of the American scene. They deal with technical and complex issues that are often beyond the comprehension of the layman. The growth of the service state administering to the welfare of the people has also resulted in a rapid increase of administrative bodies. Of course, Chicanos are often in contact with administrative bodies such as welfare agencies or law enforcement agencies. Thus, from the pluralist perspective many of their daily concerns are seen as nonpolitical or outside the realm of the regular political process.

Inadequacies of the Pluralist Model

The features of the pluralist model can, in fact, be found in American political life. However, other features of the political process, which have served as the principal factors shaping the Chicano political experience, are not taken into account. These features are of such significance as to bring into question the applicability of the model to Chicanos.

Nondecisions. There are three major characteristics of American politics that shape the Chicano experience and are not adequately taken into account by the pluralist model. First, the model does not examine "non-decisions."[5] Office holders and political influentials have structured the political arena in such a way that the issues with which Chicanos are primarily concerned are excluded or ignored.[6] Historically, the entire political process has functioned to eliminate or minimize Chicano participation and input.[7] In other words, there has not been and is not now equal access to decision makers for Chicanos.

Exclusion of Chicanos. A second neglected factor is that the boundaries of the political system have not extended to the Chicano community. A great many decision makers and influentials have not perceived Chicanos as legitimate political participants.[8] Major political parties have not responded to Chicanos for this reason.[9]

Reinforcing power relationships. A third factor, and one which is directly linked to those mentioned above, is that existing power relationships reinforce themselves and perpetuate the exclusion of Chicanos and other minorities from decision-making arenas. An excellent example of this can be seen in the Los Angeles practice of arranging voting districts so as to give little or no Chicano representation in local, state, and national offices.[10]

These reinforcing power relationships are further enhanced by the role of bureaucracies and semi-independent and independent agencies in policy making. These institutions engage in policy making, and they do so usually beyond the reach of all but the most organized interest groups.[11] Such interest groups seldom if ever articulate Chicano demands, and the institutions themselves have few, if any, Chicano officials or systematic Chicano input.[12] The pluralistic model described earlier does not take into account these structural arrangements and how they have systematically reinforced the exclusion of Chicanos from decision making.

From the Chicano perspective, therefore, it is clear that the pluralistic model is inadequate to fully explain the realities of American political life. The major problem Chicanos confront are not easily accommodated by the model.

The Elitist Model

Political scientists are increasingly explaining the distribution of power in America through the use of elitist models.[13] This is a very different view of the distribution of power in America, not in keeping with the democratic tradition as is the pluralist model.

Inequality

The basic difference between elitist and pluralist models is the lack of any kind of equality in the former. In the elitist model of society there is a division between a few people with power and the basically powerless masses. Only a small number of people are engaged in the decision-making process and the allocation of society's resources. Moreover, the few who govern are not typical of the masses. They are set apart by distinguishing social, cultural, economic, or ethnic characteristics.

Closed Ranks

The elite ranks are also relatively closed. There is sometimes some movement of nonelites to the elite level, but it is slow if continuous. This movement helps to preserve the stability of the system by preventing the build-up of stresses and strains. However, only those nonelites who accept the basic elite values are admitted to their ranks. The elites are alike in that they agree on the basic values of the social system and are mutually concerned with the preservation of the status quo. The elites are subject to little direct influence from the masses, who are largely apathetic. The elites influence and ultimately control the masses, rather than vice versa as in democratic theory.

Change Controlled by Elites

Policy in an elite system equals the interests and demands of the elites, not of the masses. Changes in policy come about as a result of redefinitions of values and resources by the elites. Demands presented to the decision makers which fall outside the shared and accepted values of the elites are ignored or otherwise suppressed. This is essentially a conservative situation and features incremental changes in policy. Institutions are seldom if ever changed and then only modified in a minor way; most importantly, the power distribution in society is never changed. Changes in the political system come about when events threaten the system and the elites respond by instituting reforms to preserve the system and their position in it. Competition is not open to everyone as it is in the pluralist system, but instead is very tightly controlled and defined by the power elite.

Powerless Masses

The masses play a very minor role in this system. They are viewed as largely passive, apathetic, and ill-informed. Mass opinion does not influence public decision making—on the contrary, it is manipulated by the elites. Democratic norms and institutions such as elections, pressure groups, and party participation do not enable the masses to govern. These democratic institutions are largely of symbolic value, serving to tie the masses to the system under the guise of participation. In actuality they have very little if any effect on the decisions that are made.

Although to many Americans the difference between these models is of great significance, to Chicanos there is little difference between the two. Under either system, Chicanos have been effectively disconnected from the centers of power. However, the probability of Chicanos' achieving their objectives is much more remote if elitist theorists are correct than if the pluralists are closer to the truth. Altering the distribution of power in an elitist system would require a tremendous amount of resources and the employment of radical, if not revolutionary, strategies.

The Internal Colonialism Model

Dissatisfied with the explanatory power of these two models, some Chicano social scientists have adopted a third model, "internal colonialism," which they feel most accurately describes the Chicano's place in the American political system.[14] This model is an expansion and modification of classic colonialism, adapted to accommodate the unique situation of Chicanos in the United States.

The concept of colonialism is of course a very complex one with with many variations, but a feature essential to all models of colonialism is a situation in which one group of people dominate and exploit another. Generally, these relations occur between culturally different groups. One major difference between internal and classic colonialism is that in the internal situation the colonized population has the same formal legal status as the colonizers.

Internal Colonialism Compared to Elitism

The internal colonialism model resembles the elitist model greatly (in fact it can be considered one variant of this explanation), but it includes several dimensions other elitist models do not consider. Both models emphasize elite control and manipulation of the masses. The internal colonialism model emphasizes the unique historical factors such as racism that have shaped the Chicano experience. It also stresses the differences between Chicanos and other groups in American society.

Basic to the model is the acceptance of the fact that the present disadvantaged position of the Chicano is the result of past oppression by the dominant Anglo (white, English-speaking) society. Moreover, the oppression continues today. The most striking political feature of this model is the *powerlessness* of the Chicano people. Chicanos lack control over the political institutions and the political process. They are instead controlled and oppressed by the ruling Anglo elite. The system is a *closed* system featuring inequality of resources and inequality of influence. These superior-subordinate relationships are not grounded in any behavior of the Chicano people—they are a function of external causes, namely the oppression by the Anglo society.

Characteristics of Internal Colonialism

There are four major characteristics of the internal colonial model: forced entry, cultural genocide, external administration, and racism.

Forced entry. In an internal colonial situation the colonized group has entered the dominant society involuntarily, through a *forced* process. Thus, they are not members of the system through choice. The people who became the first Chicanos were conquered during the war beginning in 1846 between Mexico and the United States. The territory in which they lived, formerly a part of Spain and later of Mexico, became a part of the United States, and these former Mexicans nominally became American citizens.

Cultural genocide. A second feature is that the colonizing power carries out deliberate policies to constrain, transform, or destroy the native values, orientations, and ways of life of the colonized peoples. In the case of Chicanos, attempts are made to make them ashamed of their ways, their traditions, their values; to force them to renounce their native Spanish language and take on the colonizers' English language. In short, a systematic policy of "cultural genocide" begins.[15]

External administration. Members of the colonized group tend to be administered and managed by representatives of the dominant group, not by people of their own choosing. As in the elite system, some of the native people are allowed to administer to their people, but they are usually in a subordinate position and include only those individuals who are acceptable to the colonizing elite.

Racism. The conquered group is seen as distinctively different and inferior by nature. Negative stereotyping is employed to discredit the features of the conquered group. The conquered people are exploited; they are used by the society. They provide, for example, the labor for the colonizers and yet reap very little benefit from their own labor. They are controlled, limited in their activities, and oppressed both socially and psychologically. This racism is both individual and institutional. Not all or even a majority of individual members of the dominant elite may harbor prejudiced feelings, but certainly many members are racist in their thoughts and actions.

Even when individual-level racism is not particularly evident, *institutional* racism is a dominant feature of an internal colony. Institutional racism is more subtle and much more treacherous and difficult to combat than is individual racism. In this form, racism is built into the ongoing processes and organized modes of behavior within the society.[16] Over the years the effect of individual racism has embedded itself in the conduct of affairs so that the regular day-to-day operation of our political as well as educational, economic, and cultural institutions continually puts the colonized group at a disadvantage, if not excluding them entirely.

Possibilities for Change

The internal colonialism model thus asserts that there exist conditions significantly different from those described in the other models, and the tactics for bringing about change under such a system are also different. Most significantly, change in the objective conditions of Chicanos—in health, in educational achievement, in political organization—will come only after Chicanos undergo major structural and psychological changes; that is, only after Chicanos decolonize themselves. Only after Chicanos develop a group identity and group consciousness will they be able to combat America's colonial structures. Unless Chicanos bring about such changes in their own community, the model assumes that there will be no significant changes in the basic relationship between the colonizing elite and the colonized Chicano.

Therefore, a primary objective of Chicanos using this model as a guide to action is community control over those processes which affect their lives. The goals are not participation in the politics of accommodation or individual political or economic success. It is a group-oriented drive for control over their own lives.

In any case, if the internal colonial model is accurate, little substantial change in the condition of the Chicano will occur under this system. Policy changes will be minor and incremental, if they occur at all. The basic distribution of power between the superior colonizing elite and the subordinated colonized people will remain largely unaffected. The tactics employed to change the situation then must be to change the system entirely. They must include radical if not revolutionary goals and strategies. The usual politics of accommodation will have little if any effect on this system.

To many people, the internal colonial model is unacceptable—they deny that it is an accurate description of American politics, and in any case they find its ideas distasteful. However, as the following discussion of Chicano political history illustrates, this model convincingly describes many major aspects of the Chicano experience.

Chapter 1 Notes

1. C. Wright Mills, *The Power Elite* (New York: Oxford University Press, 1956). See also G. William Domhoff, *Who Rules America?* (Englewood Cliffs, N.J.: Prentice-Hall, 1967); Floyd Hunter, *Top Leadership U.S.A.* (Chapel Hill: University of North Carolina Press, 1959); Gabriel Kolko, *Wealth and Power in America* (New York: Praeger Publishers, 1962).

2. Tomas Almaguer, "Toward the Study of Chicano Colonialism," *Aztlan* 2, no. 1 (Spring 1971): 7-20; Mario Barrera, Carlos Muñoz, and Charles Ornelas, "The Barrio as an Internal Colony," in *People and Politics in Urban Society: Urban Affairs Annual Review,* vol. 6., ed. Harlan Hahn (Beverly Hills: Sage, 1972); Guillermo V. Flores, "Race and Culture in the Internal Colony: Keeping the Chicano in His Place," in *Structures of Dependency*, ed. Frank Bonilla and Robert Girling (Stanford University: Institute of Political Studies, 1973), pp. 189-222; Joan Moore, "Colonialism: The Case of the Mexican American," *Social Problems* 17 (Spring 1970): 463-72; Robert Blauner, "Internal Colonialism and Ghetto Revolt," *Social Problems* 16 (Spring 1969): 393-408.

3. See, for example, Robert Dahl, *Pluralistic Democracy in the United States* (Chicago: Rand McNally, 1967); and Dahl, *A Preface to Democratic Theory* (University of Chicago Press, 1956).

4. These characteristics are extracted from descriptions of pluralism found in David Truman, *The Governmental Process* (New York: Alfred A. Knopf, 1951); Darryl Baskin, "American Pluralism: Theory, Practice and Ideology,"

Journal of Politics (Feb. 1970): 71-85; and Thomas R. Dye and L. Harmon Zeigler, *The Irony of Democracy* (North Scituate, Mass.: Duxbury Press, 1975).

5. Peter Bachrach and Morton S. Baratz, "Two Faces of Power," *American Political Science Review* 56 (December 1962): 947-952.

6. For an example of how these types of issues are ignored see Michael Parenti, "Power and Pluralism: A View from the Bottom," *Journal of Politics* 32 (August 1970): 501-530.

7. Rudolph O. de la Garza, "De donde vienes y donde vas?" in *Chicanos as We See Ourselves,* ed. Arnulfo Trejo (University of Arizona Press, 1976).

8. Edward Banfield, *Big City Politics* (New York: Random House, 1965) describes how this has been effected in El Paso, Texas.

9. Armando Rendon, *Chicano Manifesto*, Collier Books (New York: Macmillan, 1972).

10. California State Advisory Committee to the United States Commission on Civil Rights, *Political Participation of Mexican Americans in California*, August 1971.

11. David T. Stanley, Dean E. Mann, and Jameson W. Drig, *Men Who Govern: A Biographical Profile of Federal Political Executives* (Washington, D.C.: Brookings Institution, 1967); Charles Peters and John Rothchild, *Inside the System* (New York: Praeger, 1973).

12. Rudolph Gomez, "Mexican Americans in American Bureaucracy," in *Mexican Americans: Political Power, Influence or Resource,* ed. Frank Baird (Lubbock, Texas: Texas Tech University Press, 1976).

13. Dye and Zeigler, *Irony of Democracy*; Domhoff, *Who Rules America?*; Mills, *The Power Elite*; Morton Mintz and Jerry S. Cohen, *America, Inc.*: *Who Owns and Operates the United States?* (New York: Dell, 1971).

14. Tomas Almaguer, "Toward the Study of Chicano Colonialism," *Aztlan* 2, no. 1 (Spring 1971): 7-20; Barrera, Muñoz, and Ornelas, "The Barrio as an Internal Colony,"; Guillermo V. Flores, "Race and Culture in the Internal Colony: Keeping the Chicano in His Place," in *Structures of Dependency*, ed. Bonilla and Girling, pp. 189-222; Joan Moore, "Colonialism: The Case of the Mexican American," *Social Problems* 17 (Spring 1970): 463-72; Robert Blauner, "Internal Colonialism and Ghetto Revolt," *Social Problems* 16 (Spring 1969): 393-408.

15. Albert Memmi, *The Colonizer and the Colonized* (New York: Orion Press, 1965) discusses this process in the classical colonial situation. The Chicano

experience is vividly described in Carey McWilliams, *North From Mexico* (New York: Greenwood Press, 1968).

16. Louis L. Knowles and Kenneth Prewitt, eds., *Institutional Racism in America*. (Englewood Cliffs, N.J.: Prentice-Hall [Spectrum Books], 1969). Although their study focuses on the black experience, the process affects Chicanos in comparable ways.

Chicano Identity:

"Cara vemos, Corazon no sabemos."*

Questions that must be answered in the earliest stage of any discussion about Chicano politics are: "Who *is* the Chicano? What does 'Chicano' mean?" The term is somewhat controversial among those to whom it may be applied and is still puzzling to a great many persons in the general society. The term Chicano has only recently gained currency in the media and Anglo society, yet it has been used by Mexican Americans for generations and has become increasingly widespread among them in the last decade.[1] Moreover, during these last ten years the meaning of Chicano has changed radically. And as the people called "Chicanos" have become significant political actors, the word has entered the American political vocabulary.

History of "Chicano"

The origins of the term Chicano are unclear. Perhaps the most popular explanation is that the Nahuatl or Aztec pronunciation of the word describing the people living in Mexico is *Mexicano,* pronounced by the Aztec "Mechicano." Thus the term "Mechicano" eventually became shortened to "Chicano." In modern times, however, Americans of Mexican descent had used the word pejoratively to identify lower-class, less-educated Mexican Americans.[2] During the 1960s, the term Chicano began to be applied to all Spanish-surnamed people of the Southwest who had previously been labeled Mexican American, Spanish American, Latin American, Americans of Mexican or Spanish descent, etc.[3] Not all members of these groups, however, identify themselves as Chicanos because of the historical and contemporary connotations of the term. We will use the terms Chicano and Mexican American interchangeably throughout the book.

---

*"Though we may see the face, we do not know the heart."

"Chicano" as Used Today

In its contemporary usage, Chicano has ideological and cultural connotations. Chicano was initially a term of self-identification used by those persons who were most actively challenging the subordinate position of the Mexican American people in the United States. The term has thus been associated with all Mexican American militant and separatist groups. The term had also been used increasingly by Americans of Mexican and Spanish ancestry who are proud of their cultural heritage and wish to retain it, although avoiding some of the tactics of the more militant groups. Thus today all Mexican Americans who are working to change the inferior socioeconomic and political status of the Mexican American people, and who proudly refuse to abandon their cultural heritage should be considered Chicanos.

Political Meaning

The political significance of the term Chicano is difficult to overemphasize. It suggests a unity and cohesiveness that has not characterized prior Mexican American political activity—but which is essential to attaining political influence.[4] Instead of emphasizing regional and cultural differences—as did such labels as Mexican American, Spanish American, Latin American, and Mexican—Chicano and *Chicanismo* (a feeling of pride in Chicano heritage and culture) emphasize common experiences and serve to unite all people of Mexican/Spanish ancestry residing in the United States.[5] The term thus affects the political behavior and development of Chicanos as well as the relationship between Chicanos and other groups.

Meaning for Self-Identification

The impact of the term is equally significant in the actual development of individual self-identification and group-level consciousness.[6] As marginal people, Americans of Mexican descent have experienced identity problems that surely were intensified by the confusing variety of labels applied to them.[7]

Worse than the labels were the stereotypes used by Anglo America to describe them.[8] The Chicano has been presented over and over again as the lazy, sleeping Mexican attired in peasant clothes with a sombrero pulled down leaning against a saguaro cactus or an adobe hut. The other most common stereotype, of course, is the Chicano *bandido*. In any case, this mythical Chicano is almost always untrustworthy, lazy, sleepy, dirty, sneaky, and greasy.

In the schools Chicano children have been told not to speak their ancestral language, usually still spoken by their parents or grandparents.[9] They find no mention of the accomplishments of their ancestors in the building of this country. In short they are made to feel inferior to members of the Anglo core culture (the white, middle-class mainstream of American society). Identifying with the Chicano movement, with its emphasis on pride of culture, can help an individual overcome these feelings of inferiority or low self-esteem.[10]

Social scientists have documented that an individual is very unlikely to participate in politics unless he or she has a fairly high level of self-esteem and feels personally competent to affect his or her own fate.[11] Thus the cultural renewal aspects of the Chicano movement, the attempts of Chicanos to build pride in their history and associate with their own people, should increase feelings of personal effectiveness and competence. These feelings in turn are likely to be transferred to feelings of increased political efficacy. Higher efficacy should then stimulate political participation, which should in turn lead to an increased pride among Chicanos.

As political movements are reported in the newspapers, as leaders are pictured and quoted in the media, as successes are achieved, as goals are attained through the system and attributed to Chicanos, increasing numbers of Mexican/Spanish Americans probably will identify with the term Chicano. Thus a beneficial, cyclical relationship between cultural pride in being a Chicano, or *Chicanismo*, and effective political mobilization and participation is likely to be established. Identification as Chicanos, then, can be understood as an important and politically significant factor affecting both group characteristics and the relationship between Chicano and Anglo Americans.

Obstacles to Identification

Even though identification with *Chicanismo* would seem to be a positive and beneficial development, there are several obstacles which have prevented some Americans of Mexican ancestry from calling themselves Chicanos. It must be recognized that racism and discriminatory practices by the dominant society have created psychological barriers which prevent minority group members from identifying with any but the dominant group.[12] In the United States this has meant identifying with an essentially "WASP" (white, Anglo-Saxon, Protestant) core culture, legitimized by the myth of the melting pot. Yet it is the core culture which has labeled the American of Mexican ancestry a foreigner, a *Mexican* American or *Spanish* American or *Latin* American. For these reasons, it is not easy for an individual of Mexican ancestry to identify with the Chicano movement. To the contrary, the need for acceptance can sometimes reach an extreme state and produce a kind of self-hatred.[13] Under such conditions, Mexican Americans may reject their culture and heritage and identify with the dominant group, placing blame on their own people for their position in society.

Divisions Among Chicanos

There are also several cross-cutting cleavages within the Chicano population which tend to make difficult a unified political movement. From a political strategist's viewpoint, minimizing the differences within the group and maximizing the group's common characteristics can provide an important political resource—cohesion. That is not to say that *all* difference should be erased, only that what the group has in common should overcome the differences so that it is more likely to attain its political goals.

Geographical Differences

One such variation is regionalism. The "Spanish American" or *Hispano* of New Mexico, the "Latin American" of Texas, the "Mexican American" of California do have different historical experiences.[14] A rural-urban split is also evident in many cases. A great deal of attention has been given to the plight of the rural Mexican American, with the well-publicized *Huelga* (strike) movement initiated by César Chávez and the United Farm Workers. However, this should not obscure the fact that these Chicanos' conditions are in many ways different from those of the 85 percent of the Chicano people who presently reside in the urban areas. Also, the prevailing socioeconomic conditions in each urban area are quite different.[15]

Degree of Acculturation

Chicanos also range from one extreme to another on a scale of acculturation to the Anglo society.[16] Some Chicanos, recently arrived in the United States, are still very Mexican. Perhaps they still speak only Spanish and have not yet taken on many of the customs, values, and traditions of core-culture America. Other Chicanos have been in the United States a long while, have learned to speak English (maybe exclusively), and are almost completely acculturated to the Anglo American culture.

Socioeconomic Division

Perhaps the deepest division among Chicanos is that of socioeconomic class.[17] The word Chicano is itself of lower-class origin, and most Chicanos in the United States are in the working class. That is, they are at the bottom of the American socioeconomic ladder. However, some Chicanos, almost always by adopting the values and lifestyles of the core culture, have been able to achieve middle-class status. Some working-class Chicanos see these people as being sellouts (*vendidos*) or "*tio tacos*." They feel that any individual who achieves middle-class status in the United States has done so only at the expense of leaving his cultural heritage behind. On the other hand, middle-class Chicanos, proud of their accomplishments and pressured by the racism of the core culture, have sometimes forgotten the plight of their working-class brothers and sisters and have disassociated themselves entirely from the lower-class people.[18]

The Common Ground of Discrimination

Nevertheless, as problematic as all these cleavages are, they can and must be overcome by the Chicano movement if it is to succeed. After all, all Chicanos have much in common. All of them directly or indirectly share ties with Mexico, and the remnants of their ancestry exist in one form or another, whether it be their speech patterns, their style of dress, the food they eat, or their physical distinctiveness.

Perhaps more importantly, regardless of individual differences, almost all Chicanos have been treated quite uniformly by the core culture. Discrimination against them is found wherever Chicanos live, in urban areas and rural areas, and regardless of an individual Chicano's socioeconomic position or personal characteristics. In 1974, for example, several Chicano scholars attending a social science convention in Dallas, Texas, were refused service in the lounge of a major hotel. In Lubbock, Texas, visiting Chicano scholars were treated in an openly hostile and rude manner in a hotel restaurant.

More outrageous is the recent experience of one of the authors of this text. He had been assigned a series of lectures around the state, and when he checked out a university car from the motor pool he was assigned one of the smallest, oldest autos, with several large dents in it. He thought little of it until an elderly Chicano gentleman, second in command at the university's motor pool, offered his apologies. In Spanish he remarked, "I'm sorry we can't give you a better car, professor, The boss [an Anglo] won't let us check out the good cars to our people. He says 'Mexicans' don't take care of them."

If Chicano professionals experience incidents such as these, it is not difficult to imagine the abuse, rudeness, and disrespect experienced by less fortunate Chicanos. Therefore, a reaction to their treatment by Anglo Americans is an important common bond for all Chicanos.

The Chicano movement is expanding in scope and in depth in subtle and various ways. It manifests itself in various forms, but in each shape the shared characteristics are becoming clearer and clearer. More and more persons of Spanish and Mexican ancestry are identifying themselves proudly as Chicanos. This new pride in identification among several million people is bound to have political as well social, cultural, and economic significance.

The Chicano political movement, long overdue, is underway. How this movement has developed and where it may lead will be discussed in later sections of this book.

Chapter 2 Notes

1. John Womack, "Who are the Chicanos?," *New York Review of Books*, 31 August 1972.

2. Interviews and discussions with numerous Mexican Americans in their forties or older inevitably touch on the origins of the term. The respondents invariably indicate that to them Chicano has meant "bum" or "hood" or something similar. Therefore they want nothing to do with any group that calls itself Chicano, much less to be considered a Chicano.

3. A discussion of these labels and the role they have played in the Mexican American community can be found in Leo Grebler, Joan Moore, and

Ralph Guzman, *The Mexican American People* (New York: Free Press, 1970), pp. 385-387.

4. Rudolph O. de la Garza, "De donde vienes y adonde vas?" in *Chicanos As We See Ourselves*, ed. Arnulfo Trejo (University of Arizona Press, 1976).

5. Deluvina Hernandez, "La Raza Satellite System," *Aztlan* 1 (Spring 1970): 13-36.

6. Sidney Verba and Norman H. Nie, *Participation in America* (New York: Harper & Row, 1972).

7. Descriptions of the marginality of Mexican Americans can be found in Octavio Paz, *The Labyrinth of Solitude*, and Enrique Hank Lopez, "Back to Bachimba," in *The Chicanos*, ed. Ed Ludwig and James Santibanez (Baltimore: Penguin Books, 1971), pp. 271-280; and in Richard Rodriguez, "On Becoming a Chicano," *Saturday Review*, 5 February 1975, pp. 46-49.

8. Tomas Martinez, "Advertizing and Racism: The Case of the Mexican American," *El Grito* 2, no. 4 (Summer 1969); Armando Rendon, *Chicano Manifesto* (New York: Macmillan, 1970), pp. 42-57.

9. Thomas P. Carter, *Mexican Americans in School: A History of Educational Neglect* (Princeton: Entrance Examination Board, 1970).

10. Herbert Hirsch, "Political Scientists and Other Camaradas: Academic Myth-Making and Racial Stereotypes," in *Chicanos and Native Americans: The Territorial Minorities*, ed. Rudolph O. de la Garza et al. (Englewood Cliffs, N.J.: Prentice-Hall, 1973), pp. 10-22.

11. Stanley Renshon, "The Psychological Origins of Political Efficacy: The Need for Personal Control," paper presented at the 1972 annual meeting of the American Political Science Association, Washington, D.C., September 5-9, 1972.

12. Albert Memmi, *The Colonizer and the Colonized* (New York: Orion Press, 1965). This phenomenon is also powerfully described in *The Autobiography of Malcolm X* (New York: Grove Press, 1964).

13. Memmi, *The Colonizer and the Colonized*; Edgar Litt, *Ethnic Politics in America* (Glenview, Illinois: Scott, Foresman, 1970), pp. 32-33.

14. Joan Moore, "Internal Colonialism: The Case of the Mexican American," *Social Forces* 7 (Spring 1970): 463-472. Rodolfo Acuña, *Occupied America* (San Francisco: Chandler Press, 1972).

15. Grebler, Moore, and Guzman, *Mexican American People*; de la Garza, "De donde vienes."

16. Grebler, Moore, and Guzman, *Mexican American People.*

17. Grebler, Moore and Guzman, *Mexican American People*, pp. 295-442.

18. This is particularly evident in regard to Chicano leaders of the past. See Grebler, Moore, and Guzman, *Mexican American People*, pp. 551-554. See also James B. Watson and Julian Samora, "Subordinate Leadership in a Bicultural Community: An Analysis," *American Sociological Review* 19 (1954): 413-421.

Chicano Political Culture:

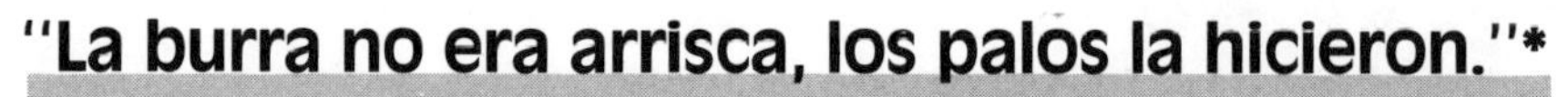

"La burra no era arrisca, los palos la hicieron."*

What does it mean to be a Chicano in late twentieth-century America? Perhaps the best way to answer this question is to examine the political culture of the Mexican American people. In that way we can gain insight into the history, culture, and contemporary experiences of Chicanos. Unless we know how Chicanos think and feel about themselves and the American political system, we will be unable to interpret accurately the meaning of Chicano political behavior.

Political culture is the combination of politically relevant attitudes, beliefs, and values held by a group or community—a group's orientation toward politics and government. The value of this concept is that it combines the historical memory of a group with the contemporary experiences of individuals, helping to explain the political philosophy and behavior of that group.[1] To understand the Chicano today, therefore, we must begin with a review of the historical memory of Mexican Americans and then combine this with data describing contemporary attitudes and Chicano experiences.

The Historical Dimension

Many social scientists and historians have disregarded or ignored the political history of the Mexican American people.[2] However, recent research documents in detail the richness and variety of Chicano political experiences since 1848.[3] Because of the existence of these other materials, here we will limit ourselves to a brief overview of this history, emphasizing the implications of these experiences for the contemporary Chicano. Although there is some debate as to when to date the beginnings of the Mexican American experience, we will follow the example of most scholars and begin our discussion with the Treaty of Guadalupe Hidalgo in 1848.[4] Beginning with this period, Mexican American history can be seen as having evolved through four

---

* "Bad experiences can cause frustration."

distinct stages: forced acquiescence, the politics of adaption, politicization, and the Chicano movement.[5]

The Stage of Forced Acquiescence, 1848-1920s

The signing of the Treaty of Guadalupe Hidalgo changed the political status of Mexican residents of Northwest Mexico from citizens of Mexico to citizens of the United States. The manner in which this change came about and the impact it had on these citizens varied throughout the region, but the Texas experience exemplifies how this change affected Mexican Americans.

Texas. The Mexican government initially sought and supported Anglo immigration to Texas. Within a few years, however, it became clear that the Anglo immigrants were violating the letter and spirit of the contracts under which they came. Peaceful coexistence quickly gave way to conflict, culminating in the Anglo declaration of Texas independence in 1835. Mexico never recognized Texan independence, however, and the issue was not resolved until the United States Mexican war of 1845-1848. Defeated by the United States, Mexico signed the Treaty of Guadalupe Hidalgo; with this the United States completed its annexation of Texas and much of the Southwest.[6]

The significance of this period for our purposes is that the conflict between Anglos and Mexicans in Texas that began in the 1830s continued throughout this period and set the pattern for future relations as well. Anglos, believing in manifest destiny and racial superiority, and perceiving Mexicans as foreigners and enemies, resorted to force to establish and maintain control. Mexicans defended themselves as best they could.[7]

It was also during this period that the Texas Rangers (now state police) were first organized. A primary part of their mission was to keep Mexicans "in their place." The continuing conflict resulting from that period is illustrated by the fact that the Rangers continue to harass Mexican Americans, and that many Mexican Americans still view them as enemies to be controlled or eliminated.[8]

New Mexico. The conquest of New Mexico differed substantially from the Texas experience. Anglos entering New Mexico encountered villages and communities dating to the 1600s, and well-established social and political institutions. Villages had highly developed internal organizations such as the Penitentes (a religious brotherhood), and successful cooperative associations which dealt with such crucial issues as water rights and grazing arrangements.[9]

This more developed structure facilitated an almost bloodless takeover. Rather than eliminate the village leadership, the Anglo allowed it to remain intact, coopted it and shared leadership with it. This arrangement benefited both elite groups. The Anglo gained control with a minimum of cost. The native elite retained a voice in political affairs, although their say in the economic area was considerably reduced. Many "Spanish Americans" occupied high positions in the dominant Republican party of the post-Civil War era as well as in the colonial and, later state legislature. Mexican American elites also managed to have provisions favorable to the native population included in the state's constitution. Spanish was to be used in the schools and in public documents, laws, and the proceedings of the state legislature. Provisions for amending the constitution were constructed so that the minority, the *Hispano*, could readily protect these guaranteed rights.

As compared to Texas, therefore, in New Mexico the Mexican Americans, both elites and masses, suffered little *immediate* loss from this takeover. The elites retained political and economic power. The masses retained their life style and traditions because there was no need for Anglos to penetrate and destroy communities as they had in Texas. In fact, many of these villages exist today much as they did centuries ago.

There were, nonetheless, significant reactions to the Anglo takeover. These reactions developed after it became clear that the political officials would not enforce the laws designed to protect the *Hispano. Hispanos* organized in protest and initiated what must be considered guerilla warfare. The most effective of these groups were *Las Gorras Blancas* (The White Caps) of the 1890s and *La Mano Negra* (The Black Hand) of the 1920s.[10]

California. The California takeover was something between the violence- and conflict-ridden Texas history and the New Mexico pattern of relatively peaceful political accommodation. The settlement pattern had been distinctive in California, with wide, sparsely settled areas mainly centering around missions and large agricultural *haciendas* (landed estates). In this totally rural setting there were the usual Mexican landholding elite and the larger groups of land-working peasants. Anglo American settlement in California in the early part of this period was very slow, and the transition from Mexican to United States control was fairly orderly. However, the discovery of gold in California in 1849 and the subsequent building of the railroad brought thousands of immigrants to the area and swamped the sparse Mexican population. The native Mexican elite was slowly pushed out of political activities, and the farm-working masses simply exchanged their Mexican leadership for Anglo American control.

The opening of the railroads after the Civil War sealed the fate of Chicanos in California politics. The Mexican elite were almost entirely excluded. Having almost no institutional base, as in New Mexico, the Mexican peons simply retained their lowly economic, social, and political status and largely remained detached from conventional politics. As in Texas and New Mexico, many Mexican Americans did suffer abuse and violence at the hands of the conquering Anglo, and there were individuals, such as Tiburcio Vasquez and Juan Cortina, who physically challenged the Anglo conquerors.[11] Anglo society branded these men outlaws, but in the Chicano community they have come to be viewed as heroes.

Pacification. The end of the Civil War brought to a close the era of warfare between Mexican Americans and Anglo Americans. The United States army now was free to commit its energies to pacifying the West and Southwest. The railroads and wagon trains brought hordes of land-hungry Easterners to the West. In the face of this onslaught the Mexican American people simply resigned themselves to the hopelessness of the situation and began to accept their fate. The situation remained relatively quiet until the beginning of the Mexican Revolution in 1910.

Freed by the Revolution from centuries of oppression, Mexican peasants emigrated to the United States by the tens of thousands to escape the ravages of war and seek employment. This massive immigration aroused once again the historic distrust and suspicion of Anglos towards the Mexicans and tended to evoke various kinds of repressive acts, further excluding Mexican Americans from political participation. Incidents such as the raids by Pancho Villa into southern New Mexico in 1916 and the resulting punitive expedition of General Pershing increased the ill feelings between the Mexicans and Anglos. The famous Zimmerman telegram of 1917—a feeler to Mexico by Germany to join her in the war against the United States and reap as a reward the return of her lands—again renewed American suspicions toward the Mexican American, even though Mexico showed no interest in a coalition with Germany.

In light of the suspicion, hostility, and physical violence of this adjustment period it is no surprise that the dominant mode of Chicano politics was alienation and withdrawal. This approach was not their choice; it was simply a reflection of their relatively powerless position. However, it should be remembered that not all Mexican Americans resigned themselves to the new colonizing forces, and that a minority of Mexican Americans did engage in the politics of violence against the colonizing United States. Thus alienation and withdrawal, although the dominant political style, was not the only response in the earliest period of Chicano political history.

Politics of Adaptation

By the 1920s many Mexican Americans had internalized their status as United States citizens, and a small minority had begun to improve their economic and social positions while also accommodating themselves to the political style of the nation. But even as they adapted to the politics, economy, and social customs of the United States, they continued to be seen as foreigners. Consequently, they set about proving they were "Americans." It was at this time that several organizations to facilitate assimilation emerged.

It is significant that these organizations did not consider themselves political. Instead, they were designed to function as social integrators, and they openly accepted the existing anti-Mexican views of Anglo America. Nonetheless, many of the activities of these groups were clearly political. It is only because these activities were accommodationist and aimed at integrating the Mexican American into society that they have mistakenly been considered nonpolitical.[12]

The O.S.A. The first of these organizations was the *Orden Hijos de America* (Order of the Sons of America), founded in San Antonio, Texas, in 1921 primarily by middle-class Mexican Americans. This group exhibited a desire to participate in the American system even at the expense of accepting existing definitions of the proper role (subservient, lower-class) for Mexican Americans in the United States. These concessions are evidenced in their charter.

Founding of LULAC. In 1929 several Mexican American groups, including the OSA, met in Corpus Christi, Texas, and formed a new organization that stressed harmony and the need to present a united front to the Anglo American community. Thus the League of United Latin American Citizens (LULAC) was born. The tenuous position of Mexican Americans in Texas was clearly reflected in everything LULAC did. The members called themselves Latins because that was much less offensive than Mexican. They emphasized their Americanness by including "citizen" in the group's title and by making one of their primary aims the development "within members of our race the best, purest and most perfect type of a true and loyal citizen of the United States of America."

LULAC's conservative position. It must be emphasized that during these years Congress, the press, and the public at large expressed great concern over the continued high rate of Mexican immigration. LULAC, like other organizations, tried to shield itself from these anti-Mexican attitudes and possible social and economic sanctions. It did so by accepting the system on its own terms. LULAC's bylaws, for example, state that "we shall oppose any radical and violent demonstration which may tend to create conflicts and disturb the peace and tranquility of our country." Furthermore, LULAC made no demands for any kind of ethnic recognition or cultural pluralism, but rather emphasized the middle-class orientations of established Mexican Americans and their conformity to Texas-Anglo society. Above all, they stressed adapting to American society.

From today's perspective, it would be very easy to condemn LULAC's early behavior. It should be pointed out, however, that during these years the United States was suffering from the Great Depression. In an attempt to alleviate some of its poverty problems, the government "repatriated" Mexican welfare recipients from California to Mexico. Countless Mexican Americans were among those "repatriated" during these years. Furthermore, it seems clear that if Mexican Americans had attempted any more explicit or radical activities they would have been crushed immediately. The reaction of a Texas political boss to LULAC's establishment implies this:

> I have been and still consider myself as your Leader or Superior Chief...I have always sheltered in my soul the most pure tenderness for the Mexican-Texas race and have watched over your interests to the best of my ability and knowledge.... Therefore I disapprove the political activity of groups which have no other object than to organize Mexican-Texas voters into political groups for guidance by other leaders.... I have been able to maintain the Democratic Party in power with the aid of my Mexican-Texas friends, and in all the time that has passed we have had no need for clubs or political organizations.[13]

Impact of LULAC. Attempting to assess the impact of LULAC on Mexican American political life requires taking into account several factors. First, this was almost exclusively a middle-class organization, and thus very few members of the Mexican American community were members. Second, the organization did expand beyond Texas to include chapters throughout the Southwest, even though its greatest impact was in Texas and New Mexico. Also, LULAC engaged in political activities, but it did so within a pragmatic, accommodationist context. Thus this was the first widespread organization to attempt to improve the position of Mexican Americans, however limited and cautious the effort was. Finally, the efforts of this organization may have reinforced Anglo perceptions of Mexicans as culturally and racially inferior. By accepting the Anglo view of themselves, LULAC members perhaps legitimized to both Mexican Americans and Anglos the racist stereotypes used to justify the oppression and discrimination suffered by the majority of Mexican Americans.

Politicization Period

The LULAC approach went unchallenged from the 1920s until after World War II. The war brought great changes to American society, and its effect on the Chicano community was perhaps even more profound. Following the war Mexican Americans became explicitly political in their organizations. They began to attempt to develop the resources with which to work within the system and yet make the system deal with them.

Effects of World War II. For a time, it seemed that the LULAC approach was successful. As the nation mobilized for war, Chicanos found themselves recruited for better jobs. They were drafted and they volunteered for the military, where they were treated better and given more opportunities than they had enjoyed previously. By the end of the war Chicanos had become an urban people enjoying a higher standard of living and educational opportunities that had been denied them in the rural Southwest.

With the end of the war, however, the opportunities available to Chicanos were again closed. While this frustrated and angered most Chicanos, it particularly affected the returning veterans, who would come to play a major role in future developments. They returned as conquering heroes, expecting a hero's welcome, and found instead what they had left—inadequate housing, limited educational opportunities, few jobs. Most of all, they confronted the social inequalities they thought they had left behind them, and with this many abandoned the LULAC philosophy.

The Mexican American community replaced the LULAC approach with a strategy of dealing with the system on its own terms rather than accepting what the system had to offer. In other words, Mexican Americans still accepted the legitimacy of the political process, but now committed themselves to developing the resources required to deal effectively in the political arena.

The CSO. The first organization attempting to implement this new strategy was the California-based Community Service Organization (CSO). It is perhaps significant that it was an Anglo-directed and Anglo-supported group. The CSO approach clearly exemplifies a belief in mass organizational effectiveness and the openness of the political process. It assumed that mobilization and organization would produce for the Mexican American community the political resources which would make dominant institutions responsive to community demands.

Consequently, CSO mobilized the community around issues such as health, housing, employment, and police-community relations. For these purposes it mounted intense voter registration and political education projects. It enjoyed success in both areas. Mexican Americans won office, and some government agencies responded, albeit in a piecemeal fashion, to demands for changes in public housing policy, hiring practices, and police behavior.

CSO remained very important until the 1950s, but since then it has changed its strategy and has become increasingly less significant. In part, this decline reflects the rise of comparable Chicano-run organizations. As Chicanos within CSO began to define their own needs, priorities within the organization came under question. It was over such a dispute that César Chávez left CSO, for example. CSO also suffered from the loss of its funding ties with Saul Alinsky's Industrial Areas Foundation (see p. 80) and from internal ideological battles.

The G.I. Forum. Another group which exemplifies the new strategy is the American G.I. Forum. Like the CSO, it recruited members from all segments of the Mexican American community. The frustration and disenchantment throughout the community are evidenced by the origin of this organization: an immediate protest to the refusal by officials in Three Rivers, Texas, to bury a Mexican American soldier killed in the Philippines. Segregation had long been a fact of life for Mexican Americans; that they chose to protest at this time, on this issue, indicates a great deal about how the war and war-related experiences had changed the attitudes of Mexican Americans. They no longer were willing to accept such treatment. More importantly, the focus on such an outrageous and blatantly discriminatory issue strongly suggests that the Mexican Americans now knew how to manipulate the system to their advantage.

The anger over this incident in fact reflects a much broader and more profound dissatisfaction, as is indicated by the other activities initiated by the Forum. It began serving the community by providing food, clothing, shelter, and legal assistance for needy families. It also turned its attention quickly to openly political activities, such as protesting injustices perpetrated against Mexican Americans and organizing and carrying out voter registration drives and get-out-the-vote campaigns. The G.I. Forum continues to be one of the principal organizations for the Mexican American community today.

PASO and MAPA. By the 1950s, this new strategy had evolved into an even more explicitly political position. In 1958, Mexican Americans in Texas formed the Political Association of Spanish-speaking Organizations (PASO), and in California the Mexican American Political Association (MAPA) was born. Both these organizations were formed to function as nonpartisan pressure groups to articulate Mexican American demands to the political parties and to help Mexican Americans attain elective and appointive offices. In 1963 PASO enjoyed its greatest triumph with the election of a Mexican American city council in Crystal City, Texas. (See p. 81.) Since then it has continued to exercise political influence throughout the state.

MAPA has also enjoyed success. It has helped elect Mexican Americans to office and it has influenced the internal affairs of both major parties.[14] Both of these organizations will be discussed at greater length in chapter 6.

By the 1960s, then, Mexican Americans were no longer willing to accept the system on its own terms. But they were willing to engage in open political activity because they believed that the system would respond to them if they developed the appropriate political resources. The system, however, did not respond as anticipated. By the middle 1960s there was little evidence of improvement. Mexican Americans were still grossly underrepresented among decision makers, and it was clear that the parties were doing nothing to increase this representation. In fact, they actively opposed it.[15] This realization produced new levels of frustration which in turn led to the development of a new strategy.

The Chicano Movement

By the middle 1960s it was clear to Mexican Americans that a conventional approach to social and political change produced little of benefit to them. On the other hand, it seemed that the civil rights movement and black militancy were achieving a great deal. To many aware and concerned Mexican Americans, therefore, it made sense to emulate the black example. Thus was born the Chicano movement.

Birth of the movement. It is difficult (and perhaps unnecessary) to date exactly the movement's birth, because several incidents occurred at approximately the same time, and all had a significant impact on the development of *Chicanismo*. César Chávez's pacifist efforts to organize farmworkers, which resulted in the *Huelga* (strike) of 1965 and was dramatized by their march on Sacramento in 1966, focused the national spotlight on the plight of farmworkers and rallied Mexican Americans as well as large segments of the national community to his support.

In Albuquerque, New Mexico, in March 1966, Chicanos walked out of a meeting with the Equal Employment Opportunity Commission. In El Paso, Texas, in October 1967, Chicanos boycotted a White House conference on the Mexican American and staged an alternative conference of their own. While the official hearings were going on between government officials and established Mexican American leaders, Chicano activists were having their own hearing in the barrio. All of these events gained national attention and thus seemed to stimulate and focus even more activity within the Chicano community.

An equally significant and unusual factor was the contribution Chicano students now began to make to Chicano activism.[16] On campuses across the Southwest, Chicano students began realizing the nature of their oppression, and they were quick to communicate this to their younger colleagues in high school and to the community at large. They formed activist organizations such as United Mexican American Students (UMAS), Movimiento Estudiantil de Chicanos de Aztlan (MECHA), and Mexican American Youth Organization (MAYO), and began protesting and demanding change both on the campus and in society at large. These groups are still active today.

Values of the movement. The Chicano movement differs from early efforts in that it emphasizes ethnic unity and pride even to the point of separating from white America. *Chicanismo* explicitly rejects the myth of Anglo superiority; instead, it seeks to arouse in Chicanos pride in their heritage and culture. Where once Mexican Americans were made to feel embarrassed about their language, customs, and food, the Chicano movement emphasizes the value of traditional customs and aggressively demands the right to maintain Spanish. Where once Mexican Americans sought to identify with Spanish and Western European traditions, Chicanos now emphasize their Aztec and North American Indian ancestry.

The Chicano movement also emphasizes the common experience of all Mexican Americans. These commonalities bring Chicanos together, deemphasizing differences based on region, language, and education that once were obstacles to unity. *Chicanismo* thus is able to include under one banner all the Mexican American people, whether they identify as Hispanos, Spanish Americans, or Latin Americans.

Chicanismo also challenges other basic values of the American system. Most significantly, Chicano leaders such as José Angel Gutiérrez and Corky Gonzáles (see pp. 154, 156) see capitalism as the principal enemy of the Chicano community, and they support their argument by documenting the exploitation of Chicano labor by American industry. Chicanos also reject the emphasis on individualism so characteristic of United States society and emphasize instead collective action which will benefit the entire community.

Different groups in the movement. Despite these shared basic values, the Chicano movement is not homogeneous. It includes members from different regions of the country, from different age groups, and from all socioeconomic backgrounds. Similarly, the movement employs all types of political tactics, ranging from conventional electoral politics to nonconventional activities, including demonstrations and political violence. But what is most significant is the shared goals of the membership: the freedom for Mexican Americans to live as they choose, retain their culture, and have a meaningful voice in the decisions that shape their lives.

Lessons from History

This, then, is the historical dimension of the Chicano political experience. For our purposes, its significance lies in the fact that it has taught many Mexican Americans a specific political lesson, and that lesson has been transmitted from generation to generation and is today a living part of Mexican American culture.

Mexican Americans learned very quickly after 1848 that the rights and privileges they had been promised would in fact be denied them. Peaceful protests resulted in frustration; violent protests resulted in massive retaliation and further subjugation. In short, American sociopolitical institutions taught Chicanos to "stay in their place." The lesson learned during the height of the LULAC period forcefully reinforced this reality: even if Mexican Americans denied their heritage and did all they could to be citizens and "good Americans," they were still not accepted as equals.

Following the war Mexican Americans once again found themselves believing in the system, only to experience for themselves the frustration and disillusionment that their fathers and grandfathers had known. The system's unwillingness to respond to Mexican American efforts to participate as equals in conventional politics alienated Mexican Americans as they had never been alienated before. It now became clear that, regardless of what they did, they would not be allowed to participate openly in the political process. So the Chicano movement was born, and with it came a rejection of many traditional American norms and a reassertion of cultural integrity and ethnic pride.

This legacy of discrimination and prejudice is a major part of the context within which today's generation of Chicanos has matured. Many parents have taught their children what to expect from the *gavacho* (Anglo). They have told them what companies will not hire Mexicans, why Mexicans go to jail more than whites, why they should not date whites, and, above all, why whites are rich and Mexicans are poor. But these same children have also been taught to be proud of being American, and to demand the equality of treatment and respect that is their due as citizens.[17] Thus, the historical lesson is confused. On the one hand, Chicanos have learned that they are entitled to the exercise of rights and privileges due all citizens, that the laws are meant to protect them as well as the white, and that they should have a voice in deciding their future. On the other hand, they have been shown that if they attempt to exercise these rights or use the laws for their own protection or make their voice known in political arenas, they will either be stilled or ignored.

Contemporary Political Culture

As indicated at the beginning of this chapter, this is but one part of the Chicano political culture. The second and equally important part consists of contemporary attitudes and values. These, of course, have been shaped by the historical experiences described previously, but they also integrate the experiences of today's generations.

Myths about Chicano Culture

Although few scholars have systematically and reliably studied the subject, many have written about Chicano political attitudes, and these writings have been the source of numerous questionable myths regarding Chicano culture.[18] To disentangle these myths from reality, in this section we will present the arguments and descriptions most often found in the existing literature. Then we will present more recently developed arguments and evidence which invalidate these stereotypes and more accurately portray contemporary Chicano political culture.

The myth of passivity. Traditionally, social scientists have examined Chicano political behavior from a primarily cultural perspective. That is, scholars have attributed to Mexican Americans a traditional culture characterized by fatalism, passivity, and resignation.

Ruth Tuck, for example, states "for many years the [Mexican] immigrant and his sons made no efforts to free themselves. They burned with resentment over a thousand slights but they did so in private. Perhaps their passivity is the mark of any minority which is just emerging."[19] Lyle Saunders writes of a "trait of the Spanish-speaking people" characterized by a greater readiness towards acceptance and resignation than is characteristic of the Anglo. He also writes of the Anglo's belief that man has an obligation to "struggle against and master problems" and difficulties, whereas the Mexican "accepts and resigns himself" to whatever destiny brings him.[20] This theme of fatalism or "hyperacceptance" is repeated by Munro Edmondson, who states: "Hispanos give a characteristic shrug of acceptance of death and illness as inevitable."[22]

This theme is repeated by many core culture writers. If indeed it were accurate, it would fix the blame for the Chicanos' subordinate position in the fact that their culture makes their lowly status acceptable to them. This would certainly inhibit any kind of action to redress grievances. However, the Chicano acceptance could also be explained by the fact that Chicanos have simply adjusted to the harsh reality of their assigned status in American politics. That is, they have had a history of being oppressed by the system; they have been excluded from political participation through various devices. Over a period of one hundred plus years, they have simply learned to adjust to reality. But even this explanation is at best only partially correct. As has been shown historically, Chicanos have not simply acceded to their lower position but instead have continuously attempted to improve their position in our society.

The myths of respeto *and* envidia. Rather than accept the fact that Chicanos have been fairly effectively excluded from political participation in this society, the cultural-value school of political culture offers several other traits which purportedly prevent the Chicanos' full participation. For example, the Chicanos are supposed to have an extraordinarily high respect for authority. This *respeto* is extended not only to family authorities but also to civil authorities. This trait would tend to inhibit any kind of demand for a change in those authorities or in the policies created by them.

Or an alternative cultural explanation might be that Chicanos are simply too individualistic to organize politically. Because they are so individualistic, they are unwilling to rally behind any kind of leadership elements that might emerge from the group. This "hyperindividualism" is sometimes tied to the concept of *envidia*, which is the idea that Chicanos are somehow inherently envious or jealous of any fellow Chicano who advances his position in society and consequently either disassociate themselves from that person or attempt to bring him down. Certainly they would not participate in any kind of activity requiring any subordination to this leader.

The myth of "familism." It is noteworthy that this same school of thought which cites individualism as a major obstacle to Chicano political success also states that the Chicanos' natural collectivist or communal orientation also adds to their political ineffectiveness. Many core-culture writers have criticized the Chicanos' alleged tendency to concern themselves with the well-being of their family relatives, neighborhood, or community rather than striving for individual success. Chicanos, instead of working hard and saving their money so that they can enjoy the material status and rewards of their labor, might buy things for their brothers, sisters, aunts, uncles, wife, grandmother, and grandfather. They might see their relatives over in times of need, allowing them to live with them, either in the home or in a little place next to the home. Thus the large family, the extended family, and the Chicanos' concern and support for them is seen as a drag or hindrance on the social and political mobility of an individual Chicano. This concern for *la familia*, the Chicano family, is often termed "familism" and severely criticized.

The myth of a disabling machismo. We must not leave a discussion of traditional values without discussing the concept of *machismo.* This concept is often seen as being a hindrance for the Chicano by Anglo writers, who overemphasize the sexist aspects of the concept. Actually the concept is much broader than simply a man's thinking that a woman should be a sexual object and a domestic servant. *Machismo* includes the idea of self-respect, honor, and dignity. It is a man's concern for the protection of his wife and his family and pride in the way he presents himself and his family. This concept could lead to a quest for self determination, embodied in the saying: "It is better to die on one's feet than live on one's knees." This, then, can be a source of political strength rather than a liability to the Chicano people.

Machismo, narrowly interpreted could exclude the role of the Mexican American woman, *La Chicana*, in Chicano politics. (And unfortunately it sometimes still functions to subordinate the talents of Chicanas.) But this would be ignoring the history of Mexican and Mexican American struggles as well as the current manifestations of the Chicano movement. The history of the Mexican Revolution is filled with tales of female folk heroes, such as Adelita, and their great contributions to the revolution. This participation by women has continued throughout Chicano history. Today one finds in the various Chicano movements across the United States women occupying very important political leadership roles. For example, Dolores Huerta has been an important figure in the United Farm Workers Organization. In southern Texas, Alma Mares has played an important role in La Raza Unida, and in other parts of the Southwest Chicanas continue to make important contributions to the political activities of the Chicano movement.

The myths discredited. Recent research has almost completely invalidated these traditional cultural hypotheses. Most significantly, there is no documented evidence of passivity or resignation among Mexican American voters. In fact, the most extensive and best documented study of Mexican Americans found no significant differences between core-culture members and Mexican Americans when comparing their willingness to compete, act on the world, and undergo risks in order to improve their situations.[22] Furthermore, studies have documented the exceedingly high motivations of Mexican American high school students.[23] In fact, these students have higher goals and expectations than their Anglo counterparts. Other scholars have shown that young Chicanos are not apathetic but alienated and, more significantly, they become increasingly alienated the longer they remain in school.[24] If, however, the nature of the schools changes so as to reinforce the Chicano student, it is the Anglo who becomes alienated and disenchanted (apathetic) while the Chicano takes an ever-greater interest in the school environment.[25]

Chicano Political Experience and the Three Models

There is, then, no strong empirical basis for accepting the traditional explanations of Chicano political behavior. We must, instead, attempt to understand how such explanations came into being. We will suggest the sources of these views by interpreting the Chicano political experiences from the perspectives of pluralism, internal elitism, and internal colonialism.

The pluralistic interpretation. It seems clear that a pluralistic analysis can not adequately explain the Chicano political experience. Pluralism posits an open system accessible to all groups who accept the rules of the game. This history of the Mexican American, however, illustrates that the system has not been open to Mexican American participation. Laws have been ignored or unjustly applied to the continuous detriment and loss of Mexican Americans. When Mexican Americans have developed resources to compete in the political system, new rules have developed to minimize or eliminate their impact (this will be discussed in greater detail in subsequent chapters). In sum, even if the American system is basically pluralistic, American pluralism has somehow not extended to include the Chicano.

The elitist interpretation. An elitist analysis can more completely explain the Mexican American experience. It can be shown that a few wealthy and influential individuals manipulated the system to deprive Mexican Americans of their lands and rights, and that since then these same elites have worked together to keep Mexican Americans at the bottom of the American social structure. The elitist analysis has one major flaw, however. It argues that the small elite group exploits all nonelites equally. This has not been the case in the Southwest. While it is certain that the lower-class whites have suffered at the hands of the white elites, it is equally clear that Mexican Americans at the bottom of the American social structure. The elitist analysis has one major flaw, however. It argues that the small elite group ticipated in the exploitation of the Chicano. Thus, even though the elitist approach explains more of the Chicano experience than does pluralism, it does not fully accommodate Chicano political pluralism, it does not fully accommodate Chicano political reality.

The internal colonialism interpretation. In our judgment, based upon our understanding of the available evidence, the concept of "internal colonialism" seems to describe very comprehensively the *historical* experience of the Chicano. Mexican Americans' lands were taken from them; politically, Mexican Americans have been disenfranchised or prevented from exercising their votes. When they have voted and organized, political institutions have developed new techniques to insure that the impact of those votes would be minimal.

Thus Mexican Americans have had little say in public affairs. Finally, the continued oppression of the Mexican American has been justified on racial grounds. Mexican Americans have been described by social scientists and politicians as inherently inferior and therefore deserving of their lowly status. The decades-long effort to prevent Mexican Americans from speaking Spanish is the best example of the policy of cultural genocide.

In sum, from a *historical* perspective, the internal colonialism model seems best able to describe Chicano reality. Its focus on characteristics of the dominant community rather than on characteristics of the Mexican American people highlights the factors that kept the Chicano from participating in political life. Pluralism, on the other hand, suggests that the only thing keeping a group from participating is itself, while elitism does not place enough emphasis on the impact of racism and thus can not adequately explain the Chicano experience. The following chapters will examine contemporary conditions in a similar way to determine whether internal colonialism or some other model is most useful for explaining conditions today.

Chapter 3
Notes

1. Gabriel Almond and J. Bingham Powell, *Comparative Politics: A Developmental Approach* (Boston: Little, Brown, 1967).

2. Octavio I. Romano, V., "The Historical and Intellectual Presence of Mexican Americans," in *Voices: Readings from El Grito*, ed. Octavio I. Romano, V. (Berkeley: Quinto Sol, 1973), pp. 164-179.

3. Rodolfo Acuña, *Occupied America: The Chicanos' Struggle Toward Liberation* (San Francisco: Canfield Press, 1972); Matt S. Meir and Feliciáno Rivera, *The Chicanos: A History of Mexican Americans* (New York: Hill and Wang, 1972).

4. Although we recognize that the historical processes that shaped the evolution of today's Chicano began long before 1848, the treaty of Guadalupe Hidalgo established a new political context with which Mexican Americans were forced to deal. Because it is this new relationship which concerns us were begin our study here. See Rodolfo Alvarez, "The Unique Psycho-Historical Experience of the Mexican-American People," *Social Science Quarterly* 52 (June 1971): 15-29; Alfredo Cuellar,"Perspective on Politics," in *Mexican Americans,* ed. Joan Moore (Englewood Cliffs, N.J.: Prentice-

Hall, 1970); Armando Navarro, "The Evolution of Chicano Politics," *Aztlan* 5 (Spring and Fall 1974): 57-84.

5. Cuellar, "Perspective on Politics," first developed this periodization.
6. See Acuña, *Occupied America*, for a nontraditional analysis of this period.
7. The violent aspects of this period have long been ignored or covered up. For a discussion of Anglo violence and Mexican and Chicano resistance see David J. Weber, ed., *Foreigners in Their Native Land* (Albuquerque: University of New Mexico Press, 1973); Leonard Pitt, *The Decline of the Californios* (Berkeley: University of California Press, 1966).
8. Texas Raza Unida Party, "A Political Action Program for the 1970's," mimeographed, p. 30.
9. Jack Holmes, *Politics in New Mexico* (Albuquerque: University of New Mexico Press, 1967), pp. 29-38.
10. Acuña, *Occupied America*, pp. 55-79; Weber, *Foreigners in Their Native Land*, pp. 234-238.
11. Recent studies challenge the view that the California experience was relatively peaceful. Pitt, *Decline of the Californios*; Weber, *Foreigners in Their Native Land*, pp. 226-231.
12. Leo Grebler, Joan Moore, and Ralph Guzman, *The Mexican American People* (New York: The Free Press, 1970), describes Mexican American organizations in this limited way.
13. Letter published in the *Hidalgo County Independent*, Edinburgh, Texas, 8 March 1929. Cited by Cuellar, "Perspective on Politics," in *Mexican Americans*, ed. Moore, p. 144.
14. Richard Santillan, *La Raza Unida* (Los Angeles: Tlaquilo Publications, 1973), pp. 29-36.
15. Fernando V. Padilla and Carlos B. Ramirez, "Patterns of Chicano Representation in California, Colorado and Nuevo Mexico," *Aztlan* 5 (Spring and Fall 1974): 189-234, esp. 200-201.
16. Cuellar, "Perspective on Politics." Cuellar suggests the Chicano movement began with student activists. Although Chicano collegians have played a major role in the movement, we do not agree that they were the initiators of *Chicanismo*.
17. For a thorough discussion of the political socialization of some Chicano children see F. Chris Garcia, *Political Socialization of Chicano Children* (New York: Praeger Publishers, 1973).

18. Octavio I. Romano, V., "Social Science, Objectivity, and the Chicanos," in *Voices*, pp. 30-42; Miguel Montiel, "The Social Science Myth of the Mexican-Americans," in Romano *Voices* pp. 45-46.

19. As quoted in Octavio I. Romano, V., The Anthropology and Sociology of the Mexican-Americans," in Romano, *Voices*, pp. 45-46.

20. Montiel, "The Social Science Myth," in Romano, *Voices*, p. 46.

21. Ibid., pp. 46-47.

22. Grebler, Moore, and Guzman, *The Mexican American People*, pp. 432-439.

23. David E. Wright, Esteban Salinas, William P. Kuvlesky, "Opportunities for Social Mobility for Mexican-American Youth," in *Chicanos and Native Americans: The Territorial Minorities*, ed. Rudolph O. de la Garza, Z. Anthony Kruszewski, Tomas Arciniega (Englewood Cliffs: Prentice-Hall, 1973), pp. 43-60.

24. Garcia, *Political Socialization of Chicano Children*.

25. Herbert Hirsch, "Political Scientists and Other Camaradas: Academic Myth-Making and Racial Stereotypes," in *Chicanos and Native Americans,* ed. de la Garza, Kruszewski, and Arciniega pp. 10-22.

The Chicano Movement:

"Dime con quien andas y te diere quien eres."*

As indicated in chapter 2, there is a great debate over the meaning of the word "Chicano." There is an even more heated debate over the objectives of the Chicano movement, the need for it, and most significantly, its membership. This difference of opinion reflects the varied regional experiences previously described as well as genuine ideological differences among various groups within the movement.

Who Is in the Movement?

It would be possible to characterize these divisions as differences between moderates and radicals.

Moderates and Radicals

The choices available to the Mexican American people are two. On the one hand, they may work within the system according to existing political norms and accept its injustices while attempting to correct them. This is the approach moderates tend to follow. The radicals, rejecting this alternative, demand instead a complete change in the system. They are willing and ready to resort to tactics which violate existing political norms in order to attain their goal of restructuring American society. While this simplistic differentiation does lend insight into the nature of differences separating many "Mexican Americans" from "Chicanos," it grievously distorts the relationship shared by these groups. Moreover, all too commonly *Chicanismo* is erroneously and exclusively equated with the latter position. In fact, *Chicanismo* includes *both* of these groups, and the differences between them are less important than the similarities that bind them.

The Common Bond

In another manner, Deluvina Hernandez has conceptualized the Chicano movement as a satellite system revolving around a common cul-

*Tell me with whom you walk, and I'll tell you who you are."

tural core. This is the most useful and insightful overview of the movement yet developed.[1] The essence of her argument is that Mexican Americans of all social backgrounds across the country are held together by the bond of a common language, Spanish. This bond more than overcomes the differences that might arise from geographic, economic, or educational variations.

If language is considered in its broadest aspect—that is, as the most important means of holding a culture together, and as the characteristic that sets one population apart from another—then the significance of this common bond cannot be overstated. Spanish represents more than merely a shared language; it is a shared experience dating to childhood. It is the key that opens the doors to childhood memories, the piñatas, the first communions, the teachers who washed out your mouth with soap for speaking Spanish, the *gavachos* who always thought you were talking about them (and often you were). Spanish is also the warm environment within which you and others like you can live out your own lives unmolested by the *gringo* (Anglo American). To be Spanish speaking is to have suffered discrimination, and you share that with all others like you. They know that and you know that, and that brings you together. These common experiences are locked into the language, and knowing that those experiences have been shared by others allows you to work with them, whoever they are.

Americans of Mexican and Spanish descent, radicals, moderates, and conservatives know they have this bond, and all want to maintain its positive aspects and eliminate its negative side. They want, in other words, to retain their cultural identity and integrity and eliminate discrimination. These shared desires strengthen the bond between the groups and make the differences between them secondary. The specific demands made by the entire community focus on changes in education, police relations, employment opportunities, housing, and health and welfare programs.

Education

The issue on which there is most agreement is the need for better education for Chicano children. Mexican American families recognize the importance of education to the point that more of their children have higher aspirations than Anglo children.[2] Chicanos realize that without education they have little hope of bettering their lives. For these reasons school policies have been at the center of Chicano protests since the mid-1960s, and demands for new programs and policies continue today to be perhaps the most widespread and controversial issue between the Chicano and the Anglo.

Importance of Bilingual, Bicultural Education

At the core of this controversy is the Chicanos' demand for bilingual, bicultural education. Today, Chicano parents remember only too well how they were punished both physically and intellectually because they began school knowing little if any English. One can only guess the extent of the damage done to the tender psyches of *Chicanitos* as they were scolded for speaking the language of their parents and their culture was ignored or derogated. Such students were classified as mentally retarded or slow learners, and their teachers felt no obligation to work with them. Consequently, many students were pushed out of school at an early age, while those that remained were "counseled" to become craftsmen, tradesmen, and secretaries.

Now Chicanos across the Southwest are demanding bilingual-bicultural education to insure that their children will be taught in their native language and in time develop fluency in English as well. The monoculture of the classroom must be expanded to include the children's cultural heritage and make it a comfortable ambience conducive to learning. If such programs were properly implemented, (experts in the field such as Tomas Arciniega of San Diego State University and Thomas Carter of Sacramento State University argue that there are only a few, if any, genuinely bilingual-bicultural programs in existence), Chicano children would be able to compete equally with their Anglo counterparts.

Community Control

Since in many instances Chicanos have been able to exert only minimal influence on school policy makers, many have turned toward the alternative of community control. Control by the Chicano community would mean that parents and children participate in making the important decisions about education. More use would be made of community resources in both administrative and instructional programs. Parents and other community residents would be brought directly into the education of their children, sometimes replacing the "professionals" from outside their community. Many core-culture educators and laymen are upset at this radical idea. However, when applied to these same mainstream Anglos and couched in the terms of "the neighborhood school," "do it yourself," and "parental input," the concept of community control fits in with the best traditions of American public education.

At the high school and college levels Chicanos are making equally intense but different types of demands. Not only are they demanding the basic skills and competence which education ought to provide but does not to Chicanos, but they also insist on an education that recognizes the contributions Chicanos have made to the United States. Furthermore, they demand that more Chicano teachers and administrators be hired.

Student Activism

The intensity of these demands is illustrated by the fact that some of the major crises between Chicanos and Anglos have developed as a result of students pressing these issues. In Los Angeles in 1968 the "blow-outs" (mass boycotting of schools) resulted from the dismissal of a young Mexican American teacher, Sal Castro, and general widespread dissatisfaction with curriculum and teachers. The students realized that they were gaining little from the existing school programs and that the only way to insure that Chicanos completed high school was to implement more relevant and sounder curricula.

Their slogan, "Walk Out Now or Drop Out Tomorrow," indicated their attitudes. Their demands were typical of the demands made throughout the Southwest: smaller classes, new schools with names reflecting the barrio (Mexican American neighborhood) community, Spanish-speaking counselors and faculty, improved building facilities, abolition of I.Q. testing, expanded and improved library facilities, and improved teacher awareness of community life.[3]

Likewise, in 1971 at the University of Texas at El Paso, Chicano students took over the administration building in protest over the university's lack of attention to Chicano course development and faculty recruitment. The best such example, however, is that of Crystal City, Texas, where dissatisfaction over the educational system served as the catalyst around which Chicanos united and eventually completely took over all aspects of city government.[4] (See pp. 170-172.) Today groups such as United Mexican American Students

(UMAS) and Movimiento Estudiantil Chicano de Aztlan (MECHA) dot high school and college campuses across the nation.

Radical Demands

While the moderates and radicals agree on the demands just listed, the radicals go a step beyond the moderates in their demands. First the radicals demand not only bilingual-bicultural education courses in the elementary schools and Chicano-related courses in the high schools, but also that the Chicano community control its own schools. They not only want Chicano teachers, they want these teachers to live in the barrio. While they recognize the value of college-trained teachers, they also insist that there are many barrio residents who lack these credentials but who nonetheless should be allowed to teach in the schools because of their skills in working with children.

Chicano-run Schools

Perhaps the best example of this alternative approach is Escuela Tlateloco, which is run by the Crusade for Justice in Denver. Escuela Tlateloco is funded completely by community sources and offers a program from kindergarten through high school. The curriculum emphasizes Chicano-oriented courses in addition to the conventional program offered in most schools.

The radicals have also developed colleges designed to meet their demands. Four Chicano colleges currently exist—Colegio Jacinto Trevino in Mercedes, Texas and La Universidad de Aztlan in Fresno, California (both affiliated with Antioch University), La Academia de la Nueva Raza in Dixon, New Mexico, and Deganawidah-Quetzlacoatl (D-QU) in Davis, California.[5] These schools share much in common. They are designed as alternatives to existing colleges and universities, and they are housed in modest facilities. D-QU is situated on an abandoned Army facility six miles west of Davis, California; La Universidad de Aztlan functions out of a small church building and rectory; Colegio Jacinto Trevino has its facilities in an old two-story white house; and La Academia sits in an aged three-room adobe house.

Except for La Academia, these institutions seek academic accreditation and outside funding. D-QU, for example, is working hard to secure a $35,000,000 special grant from Congress; Colegio Jacinto Trevino officials are striving to raise $10,000,000 in order to finance the construction of a pyramid-shaped main building. Even though these schools are tied to outside funding, they have still been able to develop programs designed to meet the needs of the Chicano student. Their programs are small—sixty students at Jacinto Trevino, forty-two at La Universidad de Aztlan—and this size accommodates their programs, which are designed to combine practical experience with formal academic work. Most significantly, the atmosphere at these schools is a supportive one of "you can do it," an atmosphere generally unfamiliar to Chicano students.

Law Enforcement

Another problem on which there is consensus is the need for improved treatment of Chicanos by law enforcement and judicial agencies on the local, state, and federal levels, including the police, the court, and related officials. There is perhaps no more visible public authority than police, and their role as enforcers and protectors of the public order makes them central to all protests and problems felt by the barrios. Since 1848, the police and the courts have worked together in support of the Anglo takeover of communal lands and businesses, and these protectors of law and order showed themselves time and again willing to use violence to break any resistance which might impede the establishment of Anglo domination.[6]

Although some of the most flagrant police abuses of law and civil rights ended by the beginning of this century, the legacy of that earlier period has carried over. More importantly, in many ways the courts and police continue to behave as they did during "pioneer days." Thus many recent Chicano protests are directed against police brutality and abuse.

Recent History

To fully appreciate the intensity with which Chicanos demand changes in police behavior it is necessary to review briefly the recent history of police-Mexican American relations.

Abuse of union organizers. It is not surprising that police have been particularly abusive in their treatment of Chicano union organizers. They, as much as any factor, have prevented effective widespread unionization among Chicano labor. In 1928, during a major cantaloupe strike, the local sheriff joined with farmers to brand organizers as agitators. He explained his actions by stating that "if they were not satisfied with conditions in the United States, they could go back to Mexico."[7] A sheriff in the San Joaquin Valley voiced an even harsher sentiment during the 1932 strike: "We protect our farmers here in Kern County. They are our best people. They are always with us. They keep the country going. They put us here and they can put us out again so we serve them. But the Mexicans are trash. They have no standard of living. We herd them like pigs."[8] In San Antonio, the police chief was instrumental in breaking up the pecan workers' strike. He hounded, harassed, beat, and jailed them until finally he broke the organizational efforts.[9]

The "zoot suit" riots. Perhaps the single most significant conflict between Chicanos and police was the Los Angeles "Zoot suit riot" of 1943. The zoot-suit wearing *pachucos* (adolescent gangs) were perhaps the first members of the Chicano community to assert defiantly their cultural differences. They were thus, perhaps, the forerunners of today's separatist Chicanos.[10] The specific details of this incident have been well described elsewhere and therefore will not be repeated here.[11]

What is of significance to us is the role of the police in these riots. Throughout the several days of rioting, the police stood by and watched while gangs of sailors and soldiers attacked and brutalized the entire Chicano community. The police usually refused to arrest the Anglo attackers, and when they did they released them without filing charges. The official grand jury report on these riots illustrates perfectly the attitudes with which police and judicial officers viewed the violence: "[H]is [the Mexican's] desire is to kill, or at least let blood . . . This inborn characteristic . . . has come down through the ages."[12] The violence suffered by Chicanos during these riots is still talked about in the barrios.

Police prejudice. Significantly, the attitudes voiced in the 1940s are still quite common today. In 1960, the Los Angeles police chief argued that the Mexican Americans were a grave problem "because some of these people being not too far removed from the wild tribes of the district of the inner mountains of Mexico. I don't think you can throw the genes out of the question when you discuss behavior patterns of the people."[13] In 1970 FBI director J. Edgar Hoover stated, "You never have to bother about a President being shot by Puerto Ricans or Mexicans. They don't shoot very straight. But if they come at you with a knife, beware."[14]

These kinds of distorted perceptions continue to guide police behavior. Armando Morales' study of arrest rates for driving while intoxicated in the barrios of East Los Angeles and in the middle-class Anglo community of West Los Angeles shows a much higher arrest rate in the barrios than in West L. A. for the same number of transgressions.[15] Similarly, more police are assigned to patrol barrios than middle- and upper-class Anglo neighborhoods even when the latter suffer from higher crime rates. This paradox is explained by the perception of police authorities, who see Chicanos as crime prone regardless of what data they might have.[16] In the late 1960s in Tuscon, new recruits observed that "a Mexican American was much more likely to be ticketed for a traffic violation than an Anglo." Traffic tickets allegedly also carried racial designations identifying Mexican Americans as "M" until through the protests of a Chicano councilman the tickets were altered to include Mexican Americans under "Caucasians."[17]

Violence at the Chicano Moratorium. It was attitudes such as these that led to violence and death during the Chicano Moratorium in 1970. Again, this incident has been described in complete detail elsewhere. Briefly, the moratorium was a rally planned as a demonstration against the Vietnam War. In addition to general war opposition, Chicanos were concerned because of the large proportion of Chicano battle casualties and the increasing neglect of domestic (especially Chicano) concerns due to preoccupation with the war. Plans for the moratorium included a march, followed by a rally and picnic with speeches, etc. at a park in the East Los Angeles barrio.

Here the relevant aspect of the Moratorium is the police activity.[18] Apparently worried at the potential problems that might arise, police tried to disperse the crowd. Very quickly they began swinging clubs and charging at the peacefully assembled demonstrators, many of whom were unaware that police had ordered the park cleared. James S. Koopman, a faculty member at UCLA's medical school, described what happened:

> Everyone was assembled peacefully at Laguna Park. My wife and I sat on the grass amongst diverse people. Immediately around us were little children playing with a puppy, an older woman with a cane, a pregnant woman with a small baby and a family eating hamburgers and French fries. The program began and after two speeches a Puerto Rican rhythm group was providing entertainment. The first sign of a disturbance I saw was when some people in the distance began to stand up. The loudspeaker

> calmly assured us that nothing was happening and that we should sit down. Seconds later I saw a row of gold helmets marching across the park, forcing everyone to leave quickly. I, along with everyone else, panicked. The terrible tragedies of human stampedes in the soccer stadiums of Peru and Argentina were uppermost in my mind.[19]

It was during this riot that police killed Rubén Salazar, a prominent Chicano news correspondent. He died after being struck in the head by a high-velocity tear gas projectile that was fired through a thin curtain covering the open doorway of the Silver Dollar bar. The projectile, fired at a point-blank range of fifteen feet, could easily penetrate a thick stucco wall. It is still unclear why the police used such a high-powered weapon. Furthermore, no one in the bar heard any warnings given by police. The Los Angeles *Times*, which during the 1943 riots had supported the police, now questioned their action. "Why, above all, were those deadly wall-piercing cannon shells used in a situation they were not designed for . . . ? Who authorized their use?"[20] After a sixteen-day inquest, the coroner's report concluded the deputies acted within "established procedures."

Injustice in Court

Exacerbating these problems is the fact that Mexican Americans find no help when they protest to police officials or when they go to court. In some instances Mexican Americans have in desperation gone to the Mexican consulate for assistance. The United States Commission on Civil Rights has documented the inadequacy of existing complaint procedures as well as the systematic exclusion of Chicanos from both petit and grand juries. As a result, unrepresentative juries decide on cases affecting the Chicano community, to the overwhelming disadvantage of Chicanos engaged in lawsuits.[21] The biases of an unrepresentative jury are reinforced by the biases of Anglo judges. The following copy of an official court transcript involving a young Chicano accused of incest illustrates this point:

THE COURT: There is some indication that you more or less didn't think that it was against the law or was improper. Haven't you had any moral training? Have you and your family gone to church?

THE MINOR: Yes, sir.

THE COURT: Don't you know that things like this are terribly wrong? This is one of the worst crimes that a person can commit. I just get so disgusted that I just figure what is the use? You are just an animal. You are lower than an animal. Even animals don't do that. You are pretty low.

I don't know why your parents haven't been able to teach you anything or train you. Mexican people, after 13 years of age, it's perfectly all right to go out and act like an animal. It's not even right to do that to a stranger, let alone a member of your own family. I don't have much hope for you. You will probably end up in State's Prison before you are 25, and that's where you belong, any how. There is nothing much you can do.

I think you haven't got any moral principles. You won't acquire anything. Your parents won't teach you what is right or wrong and won't watch out.

Apparently, your sister is pregnant; is that right?

THE MINOR'S FATHER, MR. CASILLAS: Yes.

THE COURT: It's a fine situation. How old is she?

THE MINOR'S MOTHER, MRS. CASILLAS: Fifteen.

THE COURT: Well, probably she will have a half a dozen children and three or four marriages before she is 18.

The County will have to take care of you. You are no particular good to anybody. We ought to send you out of the country—send you back to Mexico. You belong in prison for the rest of your life for doing things of this kind. You ought to commit suicide. That's what I think of people of this kind.

You are lower than animals and haven't the right to live in organized society—just miserable, lousy, rotten people. You expect the County to take care of you. Maybe Hitler was right. The animals in our society probably ought to be destroyed because they have no right to live among human beings. If you refuse to act like a human being, then you don't belong among the society of human beings.

MR. LUCERO: Your Honor, I don't think I can sit here and listen to that sort of thing.

THE COURT: You are going to have to listen to it because I consider this a very vulgar, rotten human being.

MR. LUCERO: The Court is indicting the whole Mexican group.

THE COURT: When they are ten or twelve years of age, going out and having intercourse with anybody without any moral training—they don't even understand the Ten Commandments. That's all. Apparently, they don't want to.

So, if you want to act like that, the County has a system of taking care of them. They don't care about that. They have no personal self-respect.

MR. LUCERO: The Court ought to look at the youngster and deal with this youngster's case.

THE COURT: All right. That's what I am going to do. The family should be able to control this boy and the young girl.

MR. LUCERO: What appalls me is that the Court is saying that Hitler was right in genocide.

THE COURT: What are we going to do with the mad dogs of our society? Either we have to kill them or send them to an institution or place them out of the hands of good people because that's the theory—one of the theories of punishment is if they get to the position that they want to act like mad dogs, then, we have to separate them from our society.

Well, I will go along with the recommendation. You will learn in time or else you will have to pay for the penalty with the law because the law grinds slowly but exceedingly well. If you are going to be a law violator—you have to make up your mind whether you are going to observe the law or not. If you can't observe the law, then, you have to be put away.

Demands for Change

Moderates and radicals agree that this discrimination must change. They disagree only on the degree of change needed. The moderates, reflecting a continued belief in the system, ask only for increased representation among all court officers and inclusion in both grand and petit juries. They also seek to have Spanish-speaking officials in court to help those Chicanos who know no English. According to moderates, police should treat all citizens with due respect and concern, and law enforcement officers should be more responsible to the communities that they serve. Increased minority representation in law enforcement agencies is also seen as desirable.

Radicals, on the other hand, view courts as agents of the dominant society rather than impartial dispensers of justice. Courts should be more representative of the community, they say, and more responsive to the needs of the disadvantaged elements of society.

The radicals also view the police in a totally different way. They see police as occupation troops representing the Anglo "conquerors." During the latter part of the nineteenth century and the early part of the twentieth, this is in fact the function these police performed. Therefore, to merely increase the number of Chicanos on the police force would be meaningless.

> Chicanos have long complained about police brutality. The Texas Rangers, the *migra* [U.S. Immigration Service official], the local pigs are almost always lily-white. When Chicanos protest the brutality and discrimination of the pigs, invariably someone will demand more Chicanos on the police force. Bad mistake.

> Chicanos get what they want. Brown pigs must be tougher and meaner than gringos in beating other Chicanos. Now even the *rinches* [Texas Rangers] have a few Chicanos on board.[22]

The radicals demand instead that those police who work the barrio live there. In this way, they will be familiar with the lifestyle of the neighborhoods, and surely more sensitive to Chicano protests and needs. Furthermore, it would make the police directly accountable to the Chicano community. Barring this, the radicals would demand that the police leave the barrio under the responsibility of barrio residents themselves. Groups such as the Crusade for Justice argue that the police cause trouble rather than protect the people. Therefore there would be much less violence if the police merely left. Furthermore, because the police are perceived as intruders, the Crusade for Justice, the Brown Berets, and others have issued open warnings to them that they will meet force with force. The police, of course, have not left the barrios, and thus force has been met in kind.

Radicals in Texas make one further demand. They insist on the immediate abolition of the Texas Rangers. Raza Unida Party specifically lists this demand in its party platform, reflecting the continued oppressive role the Rangers have played in the Chicano community.[23] The *rinches*, as the Rangers are called, represent the worst of American law enforcement, and they are the primary concern of any radical demands for changes in police behavior.

Employment

Chicano moderates and radicals also demand changes in employment opportunities. Historically, Chicanos have been excluded from high-paying jobs. As late as the 1960s employers advertised openly that they would not hire Mexican Americans. For example: "Maintenance, 30-45, Anglo . . . ." "Neat, dependable Anglo short order cook . . . ."[24] Furthermore, Chicanos have historically been restricted to certain types of jobs. "With few exceptions only a particular class of employers has employed Mexican labor in the Southwest: large scale industrial enterprizes, railroads, smelters, copper mines, sugar beet refineries."[25]

Results of Discrimination

As a result of this discrimination and the problems Chicanos have had with schools, Chicanos are greatly overrepresented among the laboring class and greatly underrepresented among professionals, managers, and proprietors, and they suffer from unemployment rates twice as high as those of Anglos.[26] Even when Chicanos get high-paying jobs, they earn less than do Anglos doing the same work.[27] While it cannot be denied that this situation has improved over the last years, Chicanos still earn less than Anglo counterparts. In 1960, Chicano male operatives earned 68 percent of the pay of Anglos in similar positions; in 1970 they earned 82 percent. Chicano foremen earn only 65 percent of what Anglo foremen earn, but this is an increase of 15 percent over what they earned in 1950 relative to Anglos.[28]

Despite this discrimination, the federal government seemed totally unaware of the problems Chicano laborers faced. Thus, in 1970, when the bill to create job opportunities for Mexican Americans was introduced into Congress, it got lost. Instead of being sent to the labor committee it was sent to the Senate Committee on Foreign Affairs! Finally this bill was passed—the first piece of legislation with categorical programs designed to deal with the particular needs of Chicano workers. Former President Nixon vetoed it.[29]

Chicano Demands for Employment

As a result of these problems all Chicanos are demanding a change in their work situation. Where once Chicanos were willing to accept employers' numerous explanations as to why they didn't hire Mexican Americans, now Chicanos refuse to accept these excuses and press on for jobs.[30] In California, for example, Raza Unida activists demonstrated against an employer who discriminated against some workers, and the employer quickly agreed to rehire the workers he had fired.[31]

Perhaps the most insightful demand Chicanos have made for changes in employment opportunities was made by Abelardo Delgado. Angered that the most recent obstacle to employment is "qualifications," Delgado charges that only when Chicanos apply do qualifications become important. "The more sarcastic Chicanos like myself ask when are we going to get parity in nincompoop incompetents because we have our share of those in our community and we are tired of seeing them unemployed while Anglos continue to have their share employed in positions of power."[32]

Housing

An equally important demand for Chicanos is improved housing.[33] Housing is vital to the overall life situation of any individual. [T]here is a strong presumption that some patterns of poor housing are apt to have an adverse effect on people's opportunities as well as on their immediate well being."[34] As a population, the Mexican American people suffer greatly from inadequate housing. As of 1960, almost 30 percent of all Mexican Americans lived in dilapidated housing, and they were more overcrowded than blacks.[35]

Housing Inequities

Housing conditions in El Paso are indicative of the situation elsewhere. In one section of El Paso, El Segundo, there live 20,000 people, 19,500 of whom are Mexican American. This area contains 5,400 units, including 400 slum tenements and 720 family units. The remaining units are public housing. Of the 5,070 units in existence, as of 1970, 3,870 were "deteriorating/dilapidated." Only 157 of these had inside toilets, only 120 had showers or bathtubs, and the remaining 3,842 shared 791 outside facilities.[36]

An additional factor that worsens this situation is the lack of services available to the typical barrio. Traveling from the Anglo neighborhoods to Chicano areas one notices the sudden appearance of unpaved roads, poor streetlighting, poorly kept parks (when they exist) and a generally run-down look to all public facilities in the area. Furthermore, barrios have been extremely vulnerable to urban renewal and freeway development. In Tucson, Arizona, one of the oldest sections of the city was torn down to make room for the new community center. In the heart of the new Model Cities area is a new fashionable bar located in an old Chicano home. The bar is filled with college students and Anglo "East-siders"; the barrio residents can't afford to drink there. In El Paso, old high schools and housing projects gave way to a massive freeway which facilitates travel across the city but which also devastated a centuries-old neighborhood.

Chicano Demands for Housing

For these reasons, all Chicanos demand an improved housing situation. In Colorado, Raza Unida states: "We want our living areas to fit the needs of the family and cultural protections, and not the need of the city pork barrel, the building corporations or architects."[37] In Texas, Raza Unida calls for community control of housing. "The power of the bankers, land developers and politicians must be broken. Also, the community political power must extend to the appointment of managers and boards and commissions."[38] In El Paso community leaders charged that the Public Housing Authority's actions "result in a cultural lobotomy and complete destruction of entire barrios in El Paso. We need a vehicle for greater community participation in Housing Authority Programs." They called for the immediate enforcement of housing code regulations and an end to public housing projects that isolated tenants, and demanded that these tenants be given the opportunity of moving into "regular neighborhoods." They also demanded that governmental agencies provide all other services that make a neighborhood habitable—day care centers, parks, recreational facilities.[39]

Health Care

The other issue on which Chicanos are united is health care. All available information indicates that existing health and welfare agencies do not adequately serve the Chicano community.[40]

Reasons for Disuse of Services

In fact, because Chicanos do not use these facilities extensively, it has been incorrectly assumed either that Chicanos do not care about their health or that they engage in folk medicine and thus have no need for modern health care.[41] It is very likely that many eligible Chicanos do not use these services because they fear they will be treated rudely, as in fact they often are, or because the demands these agencies make are unreasonable and violate significant cultural patterns. Furthermore, most of these agencies have been staffed by monolingual Anglos with whom many Mexican Americans simply cannot communicate. Students of Professor Ralph Guzman at California State University at Los Angeles discovered in 1968 that the Los Angeles County Hospital used Chicano janitors and other unskilled workers as interpreters. Medical diagnoses and prognoses were based on these translations! When Chicanos do use these facilities, one author argues they do so primarily because they find some agencies that are staffed by Chicanos or Spanish-speaking Anglos.

Chicano Demands for Health Services

It is difficult to exaggerate the significance of this issue. One scholar argues that Chicanos are so united on this point that it could serve as a major rallying point.[42] In Texas, Raza Unida has within its platform a plank calling for "a comprehensive, federally funded National Health Program to be instituted." They also call for state-supported paramedical personnel, the construction of community health centers, and the expansion of medical training facilities.[43] In Crystal City, Raza Unida has established a community clinic which is now serving many migrants and others who are receiving medical care for the first time. In Rocky Ford, Colorado, the Chicano community also organized itself to establish a health clinic which, as in Texas, is serving a heretofore ignored clientele. In northern New Mexico, the health cooperative La Clinica provides health services to the residents of the area.

These are the principal demands made by the Chicano movement. The fact that they encompass all aspects of life reflects the extent of deprivation which Chicanos have suffered. Although there are differences between the moderates and radicals on some points, it should be clear that they agree much more than they disagree. Tactics rather than goals separate the two groups, and while there are significant differences, their importance is all too susceptible to exaggeration.

Analysis of Chicano Demands and the Three Models

From an analytical perspective, the question we must consider is: do these demands reflect a pluralistic, colonial, or elitist situation?

Pluralistic Analysis

On the one hand, a pluralistic analysis can account for many of the factors from which these demands emanate. First, conditions are improving, indicating that the system is open, not closed. Furthermore, Chicanos are able to present their demands, and this is further evidence of the system's flexibility and willingness to accommodate any factor. All Chicanos must do is organize themselves and develop the resources sufficient to present their demands more forcefully; that is, in such a way as to make legitimate political leaders respond. The fact that there has been improvement in the educational, employment, and housing conditions of the Mexican American community suggests that in time these necessary resources will be developed.

Elitist Analysis

The demands are not as easily explained by the elitist analysis. Chicanos are clearly less privileged than many other groups in society. In all categories the Anglo masses are better off than the Chicano, and in some cases even the blacks fare better. Thus, there can be no argument that all groups are equally exploited by a ruling elite. What these demands document instead is that the Chicano suffers far more from poor education, housing, and employment than do the majority of all other groups in the United States.

Perhaps the slight gains that have been made do not in any way threaten any proposed power elite. The strongholds of power, privilege, and luxury remain untouched by progress only slightly above subsistence levels. In fact small material gains can be interpreted as "policy tokenism" which buys off more significant demands for the restructuring of the major political and economic institutions of the United States.

Internal Colonial Analysis

The colonialism analysis more easily accommodates these demands. As a conquered people, Chicanos do not control their own fate–they are exploited by the Anglo community. Thus, programs such as bilingual-bicultural education are opposed not for pedagogical reasons but because they would in fact be effective. If Chicanos gain a good education, they will be in a better position to compete with the Anglo in all areas. Therefore, to avoid this competition and perpetuate this subjugation, these programs are opposed and not implemented. The police abuse Chicanos to "keep them in their place," and welfare agencies refuse to serve the barrio for similar reasons.

Yet neither the pluralistic nor the internal colonialism interpretation is able to completely explain the problems Chicanos face. The pluralist approach, for example, is inadequate for explaining why the Chicano has suffered such extensive deprivation for so long. Pluralism demands that no one group lose the political competition regularly. Furthermore, all groups must function within the nationally established legal framework. Chicanos, however, have lost the political battle almost constantly, and Anglos have systematically violated explicitly articulated political norms to establish and maintain their supremacy.

While the colonial analysis explains why the Chicano loses, it cannot explain why the Chicano has begun—only begun—to enjoy political victory. How, for example, does the colonial example explain the establishments of Chicano health clinics in Colorado and Texas? The existence, albeit on a limited scale, of bilingual-bicultural programs also violates the colonial analysis. The willingness of government-sponsored agencies such as the United States Commission on Civil Rights to investigate, document, and charge police forces with racism is beyond the bounds of colonial analysis to explain.

How, then, are these demands and problems explained? This is a problem to which we will return throughout the rest of the book, and a final interpretation will be presented in the concluding chapter.

Chapter 4
Notes

1. Deluvina Hernandez, "La Raza Satellite System," *Aztlan* 1(Spring 1970): 13-36.

2. David E. Wright, Estaban Salinas, William P. Kuvelsky, "Opportunities for Social Mobility for Mexican-American Youth," in *Chicanos and Native Americans: The Territorial Minorities*, ed. Rudolph O. de la Garza, Z. Anthony Kruszewski, and Tomas Arciniega (Englewood Cliffs, N.J.: Prentice-Hall, 1973), p. 45.

3. Louis R. Negrete, "Culture Clash: The Utility of Mass Protest As a Political Response," in *La Causa Politica*, ed. F. Chris Garcia (South Bend: University of Notre Dame Press, 1974), p. 350.

4. John Staples Shockley, *Chicano Revolt in a Texas Town* (South Bend: University of Notre Dame Press, 1974).

5. Homero Garcia, "Chicanos and Schools," in *Chicano Alternative Education* (Lincoln: Southwest Network of the Study Commission on the Undergraduate Education and the Education of Teachers, 1974), pp. 1-17.

6. Leonard Pitt, *Decline of the Californios* (Berkeley: University of California Press, 1966); Rodolfo Acuña, *Occupied America*. (San Francisco: Canfield Press, 1972).

7. Acuña, *Occupied America*, pp. 158-159.

8. Leo Grebler, Joan Moore, Ralph Guzman, *The Mexican American People* (New York: The Free Press, 1970), p. 533.

9. Acuña, *Occupied America*, p. 166.

10. Octavio I. Romano, V., "The Historical and Intellectual Presence of Mexican Americans," *El Grito*, Winter 1969, pp. 39-40.

11. Carey McWilliams, *North From Mexico: The Spanish-Speaking People of the United States* (New York: Greenwood Press, 1965).

12. In Grebler et. al., *Mexican American People,* p. 529.

13. Ibid., p. 530.

14. *Time*, 14 December 1970, p. 16.

15. Armando Morales, *Ando Sangrando (I Am Bleeding): A Study of Mexican American-Police Conflict* (La Puente, Calif.: Perspectiva Publication, 1972), pp. 10-17.

16. Armando Morales, "Police Deployment Theories," in *Voices: Readings from El Grito*, ed. Octavio I. Romano, V. (Berkeley: Quinto Sol, 1973), pp.167-180.

17. *U.S. Commission on Civil Rights: Mexican Americans and the Administration of Justice in the Southwest: A Report*, 1970, p. 9. See also New Mexico Advisory Committee to the U.S. Committee on Civil Rights, *The Struggle for Justice and Redress in New Mexico*, October 1974.

18. Albert Herrera, "The Chicano Moratorium and the Death of Ruben Salazar," in *The Chicanos: Mexican American Voices*, ed. Ed Ludwig and James Santibanez (Baltimore: Penguin Books, 1971), pp. 235-241.

19. Armando Morales, "The 1970-71 East Los Angeles Chicano Police Riots," Chapter 8 in Morales, *Ando Sangrando*, p. 105.

20. Armando Rendon, *Chicano Manifesto* (New York: Macmillan, 1971), p.241.

21. *Mexican Americans and the Administration of Justice*, pp. 36-47.

22. José Angel Gutiérrez, *A Gringo Manual* (Crystal City, Texas: Wintergarden Publishing House, ND), p. 5.

23. Richard Santillan, *La Raza Unida* (Los Angeles: Tlaquilo Publications, 1973), p. 89.

24. Paul Bullock, "Employment Problems of the Mexican American," in *Mexican Americans in the United States*, ed John H. Burma (Cambridge, Mass:

Schenkman Publishing Co., 1970), p. 145.

25. As quoted in Ruben Salazar, "A Stranger in One's Land," in *Pain and Promise: The Chicano Today*, ed. Edward Simmen (New York: Mentor Books, 1972), p. 175.

26. Grebler, Moore, and Guzman, *Mexican American People,* pp. 209-286.

27. Ibid., p. 235.

28. Lyle W. Shannon and Judith L. McKim, "Mexican American, Negro and Anglo Improvement in Labor Force Status Between 1960 and 1970 in a Midwestern Community," *Social Science Quarterly* 55 (June 1974): 99.

29. Jerry Rankin, "Mexican Americans and National Policy Making: An Aborted Relationship," in *Chicanos and Native Americans*, ed. de la Garza, Kruszewski, and Arciniega, pp. 145-152.

30. Gutiérrez, *Gringo Manual*, lists a series of "tricks" used to keep Chicanos unemployed.

31. Santillan, *Raza Unida*, pp. 159-160.

32. Abelardo Delgado, "The Chicano and Institutional Change," unpublished manuscript, 1972.

33. Santillan, *Raza Unida*, p. 22.

34. Grebler, Moore, and Guzman, *Mexican American People*, p. 250.

35. Ibid., p. 252.

36. Department of Planning, Research and Development, City of El Paso, Texas, "Redevelopment and Improvement of South El Paso, January, 1970."

37. Santillan, *Raza Unida*, p. 21.

38. Texas Raza Unida Party, *A Political Action Program for the '70's*, p. 58.

39. Position Paper on Housing, presented at community meetings on Mexican American needs, Fall 1973, El Paso, Texas.

40. Grebler, Moore, and Guzman, *Mexican American People*, p. 527.

41. Marvin Karno and Robert B. Edgerton, "Perception of Mental Illness in a Mexican American Community," in Burma, *Mexican Americans*, pp. 343-354.

42. Jerry L. Weaver, "Health Care Costs as a Political Issue: Comparative Responses of Chicanos and Anglos," *Social Science Quarterly* 53 (March 1973): 846-854. Dr. Ralph Guzman of the University of California, Santa Cruz has recounted that tuberculosis was once the principal killer of Chicanos and that some political organization did begin around this specific issue.

43. Texas Raza Unida Party, *Political Action Program*, p. 53.

Social and Political Resources of the Chicano Community:

"Cuando no hay pan, buenas son las 'cemitas."*

Whether the system is pluralistic, elitist, or neocolonial, the Mexican American people do have resources with which they can attempt to influence the political process and achieve the ends they are seeking. The question therefore is: In view of the historical experience previously described, what are these resources, and are they sufficient to achieve the Chicano people's ends?

A group's political resources are usually derived from its social, economic, and cultural characteristics.[1] Political resources, however, can also be affected by characteristics of the entire system, which are beyond the control of the group.[2] Systemic characteristics, therefore, must also be included when evaluating the resources available to the Chicano community and evaluating the probability that they will be able to use their resources to improve their situation. A general list of a group's potential resources would include the following:

1. Freedom of social action.
2. Control over economic resources.
3. Educational attainment.
4. Numerical size and geographical concentration.
5. Social cohesiveness.
6. Political solidarity.
7. "Leisure" time.
8. Political representation and access to political decision makers.
9. Willingness to utilize nonconventional political strategies and tactics.

---

*"When there is no bread, the crumbs taste good."

Freedom of Social Action

Among the social characteristics that can be converted into a most valuable political resource is that of freedom of social action. If a person or group has a maximum number of options and choices available to them, they will necessarily have an advantage over others having a limited number of alternatives. When avenues of action or options are closed to a group, their political effectiveness is consequently limited.

The American political system has denied freedom of social action to nonwhite minorities in general and to Chicanos since 1848. Because of Chicanos' distinct cultural and physical characteristics Anglo Americans have categorized Mexican Americans as second-class citizens. As we have indicated, the overt discrimination and racism practiced against Chicanos have severely limited their freedom of action. Obvious signs of this lack of social and political freedoms include their low income levels, limited professional and employment opportunities, and ghetto-like housing conditions. Perhaps the best indicator of the barriers Chicanos confront is that civil rights laws and pro-civil rights decisions by courts have been needed to protect and guarantee to Chicanos freedoms which Anglo Americans exercise without restriction. By all standards, then, Chicanos find themselves at a disadvantage to Anglos when measured by the standard of freedom of social action.

Economic Resources

In any cataloging of social and political resources a group's economic power must occupy a primary place. Money, "the mother's milk of politics," is perhaps the most significant resource with which to influence political life. Given the extravagant cost of electoral campaigns and effective lobbying, groups or individuals with economic resources are in an excellent position to select and influence candidates and shape the outcomes of political decisions.

The Chicano community, however, lacks the financial resources which it might convert to political currency. The median family income for Chicanos in the Southwest is $8,435, compared to $12,000 for the Anglo family.[3] This difference is made worse by the fact that Chicano families are typically larger than Anglo families. Furthermore, one fourth of Chicano families live below the poverty line, while only 10 percent of white families are so impoverished.[4] These figures reflect the fact that the Chicano is at the bottom of the nation's economic ladder. The overwhelming majority of Chicanos are employed in blue-collar and service occupations—only a very small percentage are in the professional and managerial ranks. Also, Chicano unemployment is usually almost twice as high as Anglo unemployment.

The Chicanos' inability to improve their economic position is also due to the fact that control of the nation's major economic institutions lies entirely outside Chicano hands. It is estimated that at most two percent of the nation's primary economic institutions—banks, factories, insurance companies—are controlled by all nonwhite minorities, and certainly the bulk of this two percent is in the hands of black Americans. Outside of New Mexico, Chicano-owned and Chicano-controlled economic institutions are almost nonexistent.

By all these measures, then, Chicanos are lacking in economic resources. Therefore, Chicanos will enjoy very little political success if they must depend upon economic power to promote their political objectives.

Table 5-1
Occupational Distribution of Total U.S. and Mexican Origin Male Population[a]

	Total U.S.	*Mexican American*
White Collar	40.2 percent	16.7 percent
Blue Collar	46.9 percent	62.4 percent
Service Worker	8.2 percent	12.1 percent
Farm Worker	4.6 percent	8.8 percent

[a]Source: U.S. Bureau of Census.' *Current Population Reports*. "Persons of Spanish Origin in The United States: March, 1973." Series P-20, no. 264, May 1974.

Educational Resources

Education must be considered as a social resource which can be easily and effectively converted into a political asset. Education means knowledge-knowledge of the way the political systems operate in this country, knowledge of organizational skills, the ability to analyze a political situation and plan an appropriate course of action. Perhaps as important, education serves to increase the number of contacts with people who are influential and important in our society. The colleges of our nation are populated by the future power.

holders of this country, and their shared experience in college often bonds these future leaders together.[5]

Few Chicanos have the benefit of this experience, however. The median years of school completed by Mexican Americans is about ten, compared to over twelve for the core culture, and these ten years are often of inferior quality.[6] In some areas of southern Texas the average length of education for Chicanos is three or four years.[7] And in the state as a whole, 47 percent of Mexican Americans leave school before the end of the twelfth grade. In the Los Angeles area it is estimated that 50 percent of Chicano students drop out between the eighth and twelfth grade. In California school districts surveyed by the U.S. Civil Rights Commission, Chicanos were 2.5 times more likely than Anglos to leave school before graduation.[8]

This high dropout rate and inferior education combine with discriminatory university policies to keep Chicanos out of universities. In 1970 there were only 565 Chicanos at UCLA, 944 at the University of Arizona, and 1178 at the University of Texas in Austin.[9] All of these universities, it should be noted, are located in high-density Chicano areas. Such a small number of Chicanos in college as recently as 1970 explains why there have been so few Chicano professionals available to lead and serve the Chicano community.

At a general level, then, the Mexican American people lack the education necessary to deal with the system effectively, and the community also lacks the college-trained leadership that could help them overcome this liability. Thus, the community does not have the educational resources to convert into political power.

Numerical Strength

Another important resource, particularly in a purportedly democratic system, is numbers. Chicanos are definitely a numerical minority in the United States. They are, however, generally recognized to be the second largest nonwhite minority. Estimates of their numbers range from six to 15 million, with the true figure probably much closer to the latter.[10]

While Chicanos are found in every state of the Union and are numerous in many states outside the Southwest, they are primarily concentrated in the five southwestern states. Forty percent of the one million people in New Mexico are Spanish-speaking or of Spanish heritage. The four other southwestern states, their number of Chicanos, and the Chicano percentage of the population, include: Arizona, 333,349 (18.8 percent); California, 3,101,589 (15.5 percent); Colorado, 286,467 (13.0 percent); and Texas, 2,059,671 (18.4 percent). So in these states the Chicano constitutes a significant minority.

Perhaps more importantly, Chicanos are concentrated geographically *within* each of these states. This concentration is reflected in student enrollment figures. In California, over 50 percent of all Chicano children are found in three central and southern counties; in Texas, over 60 percent of all Chicano students are found in twenty-seven southern and western counties; in New Mexico, sixty-three percent of Chicano students are found in the northern part of the state; in Arizona, over half of Chicano students are concentrated in the southern part of the state; and in Colorado, approximately one third of all Chicano children are found in the south central section.[11] Many small communities in these areas are almost completely Chicano, as are many of the counties. It is in such areas that Chicanos have had their greatest political success.

Increasingly, Chicanos are becoming a more significant minority in major southwestern cities as well. Los Angeles County, for example, contains over one million Mexican Americans, and other cities such as San Antonio and El Paso have the potential, numerically speaking, to be controlled by Mexican Americans.

Social Cohesiveness

This geographic concentration is reinforced by the generally cohesive nature of the Chicano community. Mexican Americans seek each other out and prefer living in Chicano neighborhoods even when they can afford to move from the barrio.[12] This feeling of solidarity and unity has helped Mexican Americans retain their ethnic identity. Social disorganization has not hit the Chicano to the extent that it has the black American, and the Chicano family remains a strong and vigorous unit, providing psychological security as well as effective communication and support. *La familia* can therefore act as a valuable political resource, both by itself and as a multiplier of other resources such as regional concentration.

Political Solidarity

The potential of this cohesiveness and unity is now being realized among Chicanos. Under the banner of *la causa* (the Chicano movement) Chicanos are increasingly identifying with other Chicanos across the region and nation. They recognize that they share a common past and future which transcends the regional variations that separate them. Thus we find urban Chicanos rallying to support *La Huelga,* the farm worker movement led by César Chávez, and rural Chicanos becoming increasingly aware of and supportive of urban efforts such as the Farah strike (see p. 182) and demands for educational change. This surging sense of unity and realization of the importance of a united effort is increasingly obvious among Chicanos today. The incentive which many Chicanos have to end their depressed situation and earn their rightful place in American society is also very strong. This determination and group consciousness are very valuable political resources.

Leisure Time

This is another resource Chicanos lack. As members of the working class, Chicanos spend most of their time simply earning a living. Also, the kind of work they do leave them little time and energy to participate in what are often tedious and time-consuming political meetings, organizations, and clubs. Another factor affecting the lack of time Chicanos have to devote to political affairs is poor health. In the United States health is closely related to wealth, and since Chicanos can not afford the medical care necessary for a cure, much less for preventing disease, they often suffer from poor health. This, combined with a sometimes inadequate and unbalanced diet, keeps the neediest Chicanos in a physically run-down state. Thus even if they had the time, they might not have the energy to become politically active.

Political Access and Representation

A very important resource that could be used to further Chicano political goals is political access and representation. Access to public officials at least will guarantee that Chicano views will be heard. If there is a representative responsible to the Chicano community, not only will these views be heard, but they will be defended and perhaps translated into policy. Furthermore, Chicano officials are in a position to develop great expertise, contacts, and information which can be of significant use to the community. Unfortunately, there are few Chicano public officials, and even fewer Anglo politicians are accountable to Mexican American constituencies.

National Underrepresentation

Chicanos hold few important policy-making positions at the national level, particularly within the executive and judicial branches. In Congress, Chicanos are severely underrepresented. The only Chicano senator is Joseph A. Montoya from New Mexico. In the House of Representatives, four Chicanos have seats. These four include Manuel Lujan from New Mexico, Henry Gonzalez and Eligio (Sonny) de la Garza from Texas, and Edward Roybal from Southern California. Thus, five out of 535 members of Congress are of Mexican-Spanish ancestry. This one percent representation for five percent of the population has obvious and serious negative implications.

This lack of representation is even more acute in the national bureaucracy. Bureaucrats, it must be remembered, make vital and regular contributions to national policy making. Decisions made by such officials often benefit specific constituencies just as national legislation does, yet Chicanos have little voice in these arenas. In 1973 there were only thirty-six Spanish-surnamed persons holding key positions in the executive branch, and no more than half of these are likely to have been Mexican Americans.[13]

State-Level Lack of Representation

The southwestern state and local units of government also badly underrepresent Chicanos. Only in New Mexico do office-holding Chicanos approach parity with their proportion in the general population (See tables 7-6 and 7-7, pp. 110-112.) The 1970 census found 40 percent Spanish heritage and Spanish language people in New Mexico, and the New Mexico State Legislature contains 36 Chicanos out of a total of 112, about 32 percent of the legislature. California, with approximately 3 million Chicanos (some 15 percent of the population), has only five Chicanos in its lower house and one in the senate. The Arizona legislature has a 10 percent Chicano membership in the house and a 14 percent membership in the senate, while 18.8 percent of the population is Chicano. In Texas, where Chicanos number 18.4 percent, the upper house has only one Chicano senator while the house contains ten Chicano legislators. In 1974, however, there were significant gains made by Chicanos; the most important of these were the election of Mexican American governors in New Mexico and Arizona.

Local Underrepresentation.

At this time no large city in the Southwest has a Chicano mayor or a city council with a majority of Chicanos. Probably the worst example is Los Angeles. Although over one million Chicanos reside in this area, the Los Angeles county and city governing boards have no Chicano representation. This sorry state of affairs is an excellent example of the "political racism" charged by an official governmental commission investigating Chicano political participation.[14] In the case of the Los Angeles area the fairly compact concentration of Chicanos is divided into some seven state legislative districts containing a minority of Chicanos in each. Elsewhere in Texas and Arizona devices such as at-large elections minimize Chicano electoral success. In subsequent chapters we will discuss how such devices prevent Chicanos from having the candidates they support win office.

So a survey of Chicano decision makers reveals a gross underrepresentation and lack of political access. The extent of this underrepresentation is probably greater than the figures indicate.

Ineffective Representation

The fact that a person is in office does not indicate how effective he or she is in the decision-making process. Simple percentages do not measure the abilities of each public official to affect the outcomes of policy considerations; they only indicate a potential. Also, the fact that an individual in office has a Spanish surname does not necessarily mean that he or she identifies with the needs and the values of the Chicano people. Our geographical basis of representation makes it even less likely that a Chicano public official will indeed consider Chicanos, rather than a geographical unit, as his constituency.

Quite commonly even though a Chicano is in political office his power base in his constituency is not the Chicano people but instead some powerful non-Chicano groups or individuals. The Chicano public official is also constrained in his political influence by the fact that he is operating under rules of the game that are usually not reflective of Chicano values and norms. Therefore, the decision-making structure in the United States has generally remained the same, even though the public officials operating under those rules change from time to time.

To sum up, once again the Chicano is comparatively resourceless when measured by any index of political representation and access.

Willingness to Use Nonconventional Tactics

Another resource not usually considered is the willingness of a group to resort to nontraditional tactics, including the use of violence. Particularly when one discusses non-white ethnics, who are relatively powerless, it is necessary to include such factors in their resource base. There is little doubt that public decision makers can be intimidated or influenced by the fear such tactics generate.

In conventional politics officeholders may be threatened by the loss of office through the ballot box. Pressure groups exercise influence by threatening to withhold support in future elections unless officials act in specified ways. Lacking these conventional resources, Chicanos have begun to use threats of disruption to wring favorable policy decisions.[15] The threat need not be directed at property or persons; it may simply be aimed at disturbing the everyday functioning of government. Tactics such as sit-ins, marches or walk-outs pose a real threat to public officials charged with maintaining a smoothly functioning system.

Violence, of course, always looms in the background of such events, and this is the source of greatest fear among Anglo office holders. Although it is not widely known, the Chicano population has been involved in several civil disturbances over the past few years.[16] Throughout the Southwest there have been not only peaceful strikes, boycotts, and demonstrations, but also outbreaks of violence, often sparked by indiscreet police activities at otherwise peaceful occasions. These violent episodes have resulted in a great loss of property and harm to many individuals, including several deaths.

Relative Powerlessness of Chicanos

The total of the various resources possessed by the Mexican American community is not an impressive sum. Chicanos lay claim to few of the traditional sources of political influence such as wealth, education, time, political experience, and public office holding. On the other hand, Chicanos do have a growing sense of identity and community. They are rallying under the banner of *La Causa,* they have a strong social base with a common language and culture, and their families and communities by and large remain a strong source of individual as well as group political power. Nevertheless, it is clear that by traditional measures of potential political power—that is, political resources—the Chicano must be considered *relatively powerless* or resourceless when compared to most other ethnic groups in this country, certainly compared to the dominant Anglo society.

Analysis According to the Three Models

Thus, whether one chooses the pluralistic, elitist, or neocolonialist model to describe the distribution of power in America, the Chicano is certainly at a disadvantage. The pluralistic model emphasizes that groups must be relatively equal in resources in order to share in the competitive push and pull of politics, yet we have seen that the Chicano does not possess an equal share of the necessary resources. The neocolonial model assumes great inequalities between the colonizer and the colonized, which is the case between Anglos and Chicanos. The elitist model argues that all nonelite groups are equally oppressed, but again we have shown this not to be the case—Chicanos are more lacking in resources than white groups.

Which Strategy?

The condition of relative powerlessness poses some hard choices for Chicanos—should they attempt to build their traditional power bases, strive for increased education and economic advantages, and make greater efforts towards electing more Chicanos to public office? Or is this strategy too risky? Does it take too much time, and are its chances for success rather low?

This largely depends on whether power in America is distributed along pluralistic lines in a relatively open system or whether it is indeed a closed system for non-white minorities. If the system is closed, then the strategies employed by Chicanos must be those of *liberation*, which will maximize those resources that they currently possess—their culture, their language, their concentration of numbers, their values of *carnalismo* (brotherhood) and the extended family, and their increasing willingness to confront the political system directly. By employing very effectively and strongly the resources that they currently possess, they could quite dramatically confront the elite in any neocolonial situation.

The mode of increasing their conventional social and economic resources such as education and wealth, with an idea to converting them to political resources in the future, should be a trivial activity under a neocolonial system. It might even be a total waste of time and effort, since these resources would not basically alter the Chicanos' colonized status.

Whether the system is closed, open, or something in between will be discussed again after we have examined how the Mexican American people are employing their resources and how successful their efforts to effect change have been.

Chapter 5 Notes

1. For a development of this idea, see James S. Coleman, *Resources for Social Change: Race in the United States* (New York: Wiley, 1971).
2. This argument is developed forcefully in Charles V. Hamilton and Stokely Carmichael, *Black Power* (New York: Random House [Vintage Books], 1967).
3. U.S. Bureau of the Census, "Persons of Spanish Origin in the United States: March, 1974," *Current Population Reports*, series P-20, no. 280.
4. U.S. Bureau of the Census, "Selected Characteristics of Persons and Families of Mexican, Puerto Rican and Other Spanish Origin: March 1971," *Current Population Reports*, series P-20, no. 224.
5. The importance of these ties is discussed in C. Wright Mills, *The Power Elite* (New York: Oxford U. Press, 1956). An indication of the closed circle that develops among Anglos from these shared experiences is suggested in Thomas R. Dye and L. Harmon Zeigler, *The Irony of Democracy* (North Scituate, Mass. Duxbury Press, 1975), pp. 103-145.
6. U.S. Commission on Civil Rights, *Mexican American Education Study*, Volumes 1-5, 1971-1973.

7. Ironically, the attainment of a median education of 2.3 years in 1960 compared to a median attainment for Anglos of 11.2 years is described by one author, Shockley, as evidence of "improvement." With unbelievable understatement he adds, "but to many Mexican Americans the progress seemed slow indeed." John Staples Shockley, *Chicano Revolt in a Texas Town* (South Bend: Univeristy of Notre Dame Press, 1974), p. 117.

8. United States Commission on Civil Rights, *Mexican American Educational Series, Report 2: The Unfinished Education: Outcomes for Minorities in the Five Southwestern States*, October 1971.

9. Racial and Ethnic Enrollment, Data from Institutions of Higher Education (Fall 1970), U.S. Department of Health, Education and Welfare/Office for Civil Rights.

10. It is difficult to determine precisely the number of Mexican Americans living in the United States. See Jose Hernandez, Leo Estrada and David Alvirez, "Census Data and the Problem of Conceptually Defining the Mexican American Population," *Social Science Quarterly* 53 (March 1973): 671-687.

11. United States Commission on Civil Rights, *Mexican American Education Study, Report 1: Ethnic Isolation of Mexican Americans in The Public Schools of the Southwest*, April 1971, p. 19.

12. Leo Grebler, Joan Moore, Ralph Guzman, *The Mexican American People* (New York: The Free Press, 1970), pp. 329-330.

13. Rudolph Gomez, "Mexican Americans in American Bureaucracy," in *Mexican Americans: Political Power, Influence or Resource,* ed. Frank Baird (Lubbock, Texas: Texas Tech University Press, 1976).

14. California State Advisory Committee, U.S. Commission on Civil Rights, "Political Participation of Mexican Americans in California," August 1971.

15. Michael Lipsky, "Protest as a Political Resource," *American Political Science Review* 62 (December 1968): 1144-1158.

16. Armando Morales, *Ando Sangrando (I Am Bleeding): A Study of Mexican American-Police Conflict* (La Puente, Calif.: Perspectiva Publications, 1972).

Chicano Community Organizations and Interest Groups:

"El que no mira adelante, atras se queda."*

The role of interest groups in American political life has been described and analyzed since the birth of this nation. All these studies conclude that individual political action is relatively unimportant when compared with the role of organized groups. All agree that the most effective means for influencing decision makers and attaining political power is through organized group activities. This view derives from the pluralist belief that the political process involves continuous interaction between distinct groups seeking to achieve specific policy goals. The interaction requires negotiation, bargaining, and compromise among the groups themselves and between the groups and governmental agencies. In theory, all or most individuals in society will have their interests represented by some organization at some time, and no group is systematically excluded from the interactions or regularly defeated in the competition.[1]

Given the importance of organizations to political life, it is not surprising that scholars have studied Chicano organizations. Their findings and conclusions resemble the conclusions which sociologists and anthropologists reached when they studied Chicano culture. They point out that the Chicano "has developed few voluntary organizations." According to them, the reasons for so few organizations are that Chicanos are so individualistic and tradition bound that they are unable to work together to achieve common goals.[2] "Some societies display a certain flair for organizing and proliferating instrumental groups. Clearly the Chicanos do not . . . . Organization of groups for the attainment of goals, whether diffuse or particular, is not one of the instrumental techniques made available to them by their culture."[3] This alleged inability to develop organizations is then cited as the principal reason that Mexican Americans have been politically ineffective.

*"He who does not look ahead will stay behind."

The Historical Overview

Recently more objective research has invalidated these earlier studies.[4] It was now clear that Chicanos have had organizations throughout their history, and the nature of their organizations has been affected by the broader national environment.

Early Organizations

Overall, Chicano organizations have developed to meet community needs that were not being met elsewhere. These early organizations included religious groups such as the Penitentes of New Mexico which also functioned as an agent of cultural preservation, and mutual aid societies which served multiple functions. Whatever their explicit objectives, these organizations provided "a forum for discussion and a means of organizing the social life of the community." Thus they served the functions comparable to the ethnic clubs in the Midwest and East (Sons of Italy, Sons of Erin, etc.).[5]

Accommodationist Organizations

By the turn of the century these organizations began to take on political functions, in however subtle a form. A period of accommodationist activities began when Mexican Americans began to go along with the biases of the dominant community, forming organizations which attempted to foster patriotism and loyalty to the Unites States and demonstrate to all that Mexican Americans were first and foremost Americans. The League of United Latin American Citizens is the best example of this type of organization.

The "apolitical" nature of LULAC is evidenced by the organization's refusal to organize a drive for poll tax payment and voter registration. Such political actions would mean that LULAC "would no longer be accorded the esteem of Anglos who conceived of the group as an educational and citizenship-oriented organization."[6] As indicated previously, LULAC was primarily a middle-class group. Thus it is not surprising that its membership was unwilling to initiate any activities which might draw a negative response from the dominant white community, threatening the shaky status of the upwardly mobile "American of Mexican descent."

Post-World War II Organizations

After World War II more explicitly political organizations emerged.

The CSO. One of the earliest and most significant was the Community Service Organization (CSO), established in 1947. This California organization was devoted to stimulating the local community to put pressure on local officials in the area of housing, health services, jobs, and police activities. It was an organization that crossed class lines and was also multiethnic. Some of its most active non-Chicano members were Fred Ross and Saul Alinsky. Of the Chicanos, the best known was César Chávez. The achievements of the CSO were so extensive that Congressman Edward Roybal of Los Angeles has stated: "I don't think that there's another organization that has accomplished as much in the field of civic awakening as the CSO has."[7] This organization was relatively successful in wrestling concessions from the local governments, particularly in the Los Angeles area.

The G.I. Forum. At approximately the same time Mexican Americans in Texas organized the American G.I. Forum. The name of the organization suggests its nationalistic and patriotic orientation. But unlike LULAC, the G.I. Forum, led by Dr. Hector Garcia, began openly challenging discrimination and called for equal rights and privileges for the Mexican American people. Dr. Garcia pressed his demands with school boards and public officials from the local level to the national. Believing that Mexican Americans could alter their situations through effective use of the vote, he dedicated his efforts to increasing Mexican Americans' voter registration and participation.

The MAPA. Within a few years of the founding of the G.I. Forum the first explicitly Chicano political organizations were born in California and Texas. The California-based Mexican American Political Association (MAPA) covered a wide range of political activities including political education, voter registration drives, community organization, and the encouragement of activity within the two major political parties. MAPA was designed to function as an independent political force, throwing its support to whichever party and candidate would serve the needs of the Chicano community. In practice, however, MAPA supported the Democratic party unfailingly and was taken for granted by them until 1970. Then, in rebellion, MAPA declined to endorse candidates from either party, and thus established itself as a more independent political organization.[8] Although MAPA is still a viable organization, its greatest successes came in the 1950s when it successfully supported Chicano candidates for the California assembly and subsequently successfully supported Edward Roybal in his congressional election.

PASO. In Texas, the Political Association of Spanish speaking Organizations (PASO) engaged in activities similar to those of MAPA. PASO, existing as it did in the more conflict-ridden and oppressive atmosphere of Texas politics, was less ethnically oriented than its California counterpart, as is evidenced in its name. PASO also included a larger base of non-Chicanos in its membership than did MAPA. PASO did however succeed in electing local Chicano officials as well as promoting the election of some national representatives. Its major success was in 1963 in Crystal City (See p. 31);[9] since then, PASO's significance seems to have continuously diminished.

Labor groups. Paralleling the development of these organizations has been the growth of Chicano labor groups. Since the nineteenth century Mexican American laborers have attempted to organize to improve their working conditions and salary. It is only natural that labor organization would have been an area of primary activity for Chicanos, given that the Chicano population is overwhelmingly represented within the Southwest's labor force. Success in this area has varied, however, In mining, Chicanos have attained considerable success, evidenced by the fact that Maclovio Barraza is head of the United Mill and Mine Workers in Arizona. Because of his institutional position and strength of personality, Barraza is a force to be reckoned with in Arizona politics. In 1972, Chicano laborers led a strike of the Amalgamated Textile Union against the Farah Manufacturing Company. After years of struggle they emerged triumphant. (see p. 182). César Chávez and his agricultural workers' union also persevered in their efforts, enduring many hardships and major setbacks in their struggle to win union victories. The widely and efficiently organized *Huelga* activities have resulted in California legislation which will give farm workers many of the same benefits provided other laborers by the National Labor Relations Act, including the right to choose union representation through secret ballots.

The history of Chicano labor is just now being written.[10] To the extent that this history is known, however, it is clear that efforts to organize Chicano labor have confronted major obstacles which organizers in other parts of the nation did not face, at least not to the same extent. First, economic conditions in the Southwest are not conducive to large-scale organization. Only recently have industrial and manufacturing firms come to the West, and it is precisely such firms that serve as the basis for unionization.

Lacking large, permanent labor populations, Chicanos have been forced to divert their efforts to construction trades and agrarian works, both of which are very difficult to penetrate and organize. Where stable work forces exist Chicano organizers have been successful, as is illustrated by Maclavio Barraza in Arizona. Second, Chicano organizers face a racist barrier which is used to mobilize entire white communities against any Chicano labor organization. The history of Chicano strikers in San Antonio and throughout California illustrates this clearly.[11] Any evaluation of Chicano labor organizational ability must, therefore, carefully weigh these obstacles.

Radical Chicano Groups

Since the middle 1960s new kinds of Chicano organizations have developed. Many of these tend to reject many of the values, customs, and institutions of the larger society, turning inward to the Chicano community. Such groups include the Brown Berets, Black Berets, the Alianza Federal de Pueblos Libres (Federal Alliance of Free City-States), the Crusade for Justice, and student organizations such as Movimiento Estudiantil Chicano de Aztlan (MECHA), Mexican American Youth Organization (MAYO), United Mexican American Students (UMAS), and many other high school groups. These groups generally reject the argument that American society as presently structured offers any real opportunities to Chicanos. Thus they have become antiassimilationist and antiaccommodationist. Rather than organize along conventional lines, leaders of these organizations argue that Chicanos should organize along purely ethnic lines, remaining separate from non-Chicano affiliations.

Characteristics of radical groups. These groups share several additional characteristics. They are composed mainly of lower-class or working-class members with a leadership corps of middle-class individuals. They have all indicated, and in some cases demonstrated, a willingness to resort to violence to achieve their ends. The Berets, a self-defense organization, have served as a buffer between oppressive police tactics and Chicano communities. They have engaged in confrontations with the police, and are vigilant and vocal in criticizing police forces. More recently, the Berets have directed most of their efforts toward self-help activities such as instituting community-controlled culture centers and health clinics.

The Alianza has attempted to regain the historical base of the Chicano in order to reestablish self-sufficient Chicano communities in northern New Mexico. It continues to stress the distinctive nature of *La Raza* (the Chicano) and maintains its efforts to raise the ethnic consciousness and cultural pride of the Chicano people. The Crusade for Justice, based in the Denver area, emphasizes cultural nationalism in its efforts. It has established its own school system all the way from grade school to college and support its own political organizations such as La Raza Unida Party. The student groups have also demonstrated a willingness to resort to violence or at least disruptive behavior whenever necessary.

Membership of radical groups. Many of these groups include members from the hard core of socially disadvantaged, the most abused and alienated Chicanos. The *batos locos* ("crazy guys," hooligans), convicts, exconvicts, narcotic users, and high school dropouts and pushouts, angered and embittered by their experiences, are able and willing to devote their full time and energies to organizational activities. As descendants of the *pachucos* of the 1940s, these Chicanos are asserting themselves and defining their own identity.

Unlike the *pachuco*, however, today's alienated Chicanos are directing their efforts at challenging and restructuring both the Anglo system and their own community. That these organizations advocate cultural nationalism and have separatist overtones reflects an awareness by the members that Anglo society has already separated them out and pushed them aside. Therefore, these groups seek to institutionalize and turn to their advantage a situation that already exists.

Effectiveness and Future of Chicano Organizations

The suggestion that Chicanos are ignorant of the importance of organizations or that they are incapable of establishing organizations is clearly unsubstantiated. What is unclear, however, is how successful these organizations have been. What have been their strengths and weaknesses? What is their future?

Low Level of Awareness and Participation

The most important question concerning the effectiveness of Chicano organizations is how much support they have within the Mexican American community. On the basis of research conducted in various parts of Texas and California, it seems clear that these organizations have had little support. Overall, Mexican Americans are not actively involved in formal organizations; indeed, most of these organizations are barely known outside of a specific region. As Tables 6-1 and 6-2 indicate, no Mexican American organization was even known by the majority of the Chicano population in Los Angeles as of 1965, and in San Antonio only LULAC and the American G. I. Forum were recognized by the majority of Chicanos in that city. Neither of these, however, had a significant membership.

Increasing awareness. More recent studies suggest an increased awareness of these organizations, even though widespread support and membership in them is still not evident. In small Texas cities, for example, Mexican Americans were more aware of LULAC, MAPA, and PASO than were San Antonio respondents several years earlier.[12]

Table 6-1

Support and Awareness of Chicano Community Organizations, Los Angeles 1965,[a] 1972[b]

Organization	*Very Familiar/Belongs 1965, 1972*	*Heard of It 1965, 1972*		*Never Heard of It 1965, 1972*	
Alianza Hispano-American	10 percent	32 percent		58 percent	
American G.I. Forum	4	20		76	
Community Service Organization	2	14	26	82	67
Democratic Clubs	10	42		48	
LULAC	4	14	18	86	78
MAPA	5	39	67	61	29
PASO	1	4	10	96	86
Republican Clubs	8	33		59	
Viva Johnson Clubs	4	19		77	

[a]Leo Grebler, Joan Moore, Ralph Guzman, *The Mexican American People* (New York: Free Press, 1970), p. 547.

[b]Biliana Ambrecht and Harry Pachon, "Ethnic Political Mobilization in a Mexican American Community: An Exploratory Study of East Los Angeles, 1965-1972," *Western Political Quarterly* 28 (September 1974): 510.

Table 6-2
Support and Awareness of Chicano Community Organizations, Texas

Organization	Very Familiar/Belongs		Heard of It		Never Heard of It	
	San Antonio (1965-66)	*Texas Communities (1974)*	*San Antonio (1965-66)*	*Texas Communities (1974)*	*San Antonio (1965-66)*	*Texas Communities (1974)*
Alianza Hispano-American	1 percent		14 percent		85 percent	
American G.I. Forum	8	3	43	39	49	61
Community Service Organization	1		7		92	
Democratic Clubs	5		36		59	
LULAC	15	7	59	63	26	37
MAPA	1	0	5	15	94	65
PASO	6	0	42	35	52	65
Republican Clubs	3		29		68	
Viva Johnson Clubs	4		33		63	
MAYO		0		44		56
Mexican American Alliance		2		20		80
Raza Unida		2		52		48

Sources: Grebler et al., *Mexican American People*; Teske and Nelson, "Mexican American Political Power."

Similarly, in California, Chicanos were more aware of all Chicano organizations in 1972 than they were just a few years earlier.[13]

Although this increased public awareness suggests that Chicano organizations are becoming better known throughout the barrios, it still seems clear that overall these organizations do not have mass support and are not well enough established and known to mobilize the community or serve as primary communication links for the community. In Lubbock, Waco, Austin, and McAllen, Texas, for example, 85 percent of the Mexican American middle class are members of no Chicano organization. Yet it is precisely this group that is in the best position to provide the leadership and expertise necessary for these organizations to succeed.[14]

Factors discouraging participation. There are numerous factors that explain this low level of awareness and participation. As members of the working class, most Chicanos have not had the time to put into organizational activities, and thus few are active in clubs and formal groups. They have also been subjected to a core-culture political education that emphasizes individual rather than group political activity. Thus, they have not been encouraged to develop ethnic-based groups.[15] Chicanos may be less active in organizations also because of fear. Threats and violence have long been used against Chicanos, and the memories of arrests, beatings, and exportation surely serve as a restraint to many individuals.

General low participation in United States. It should also be noted that Chicano organizational participation is not unlike the organizational participation of other segments of the United States population.[16] Many studies show that only a small minority of United States citizens are voluntary members of associations, and only a small percentage of these members are active in their organizations.[17] Secondly, rates of organizational activity among other ethnic groups and persons of low socioeconomic status reveal that their activity in associations is comparably low.[18] The rate of participation among Chicanos is even lower than it seems, for the Chicanos who are active in organizations hold membership in numerous groups. In Lubbock, for example, almost 90 percent of the community's leaders were active in three or more organizations.[19] Thus, not only is overall participation low, but the high level of cross-memberships suggests that the depth to which these organizations penetrate is shallow indeed.

Regional and generational differences. The varied regional and generational experiences previously described also have a negative impact on Chicano organizational development. In each region Chicanos organize groups to meet their local needs, and these organizations reflect the structural characteristics of their immediate society. Thus, in California, groups have been historically more willing to call themselves Mexican; in Texas, however, the oppression and racism have been so severe that phrases such as "Latin American" and "Spanish speaking" have been used to identify Chicano groups. In New Mexico, "Hispano" has been a predominant term in community organizations.

Overlapping these regional differences are generational splits. Older members of the community are unenthusiastic if not unwilling to belong to a group identified as Chicano, while the younger militants are adamant in insisting that they are Chicanos and that their groups are Chicano. The inability to overcome these differences so as to confront serious problems prevents many individuals from getting involved with any groups.

Thus while Chicanos have been accused of being inherently incapable of developing organizations, they in fact suffer from exactly the same opposite problem—an overwhelming number of groups. In recent years efforts to overcome this problem through the establishment of unity councils in California, Texas, Colorado, and the Southwest in general have had mixed results. The Chicano community realizes, nonetheless, that they need to overcome this fragmentation, and efforts to do so are continuing.

Lack of national organizations. These regional and generational differences have also been a major obstacle preventing national Chicano organizations from developing.[20] Unable to agree on what to call themselves, these groups are unlikely to be able to come together to solve problems that require delicate bargaining and compromise. Until Raza Unida was established, there was no national organization, and it is uncertain whether even Raza Unida can be considered a genuinely national group. Clearly a major factor inhibiting the development of a Chicano equivalent to the NAACP or the Urban League is the fact that Chicano organizations simply do not have the resources to develop and maintain a national group. Except for the Southwest Council of La Raza, founded in 1968, Chicano organizations must depend on volunteer staff, and such help is hardly sufficient to develop and maintain an effective national organization.

Guidelines for More Effective Organization

If Chicano organization is to be more effective in the future, there are several guidelines that might be followed. Miguel Tirado has described some of the characteristics of those Chicano organizations that have been successful.[21]

Multifunctional and family-oriented nature. First, a successful organization will more than likely be multifunctional in nature; it is doubtful than an effective organization can be only cultural or only political or only economic—it must be a combination of all of these. Second, the organization must conform to Chicano values; one of the most important of these is the role of the family. Organizations must be designed to involve the whole family, wives, children, and other relatives, rather than only the adult males.

Crisis as catalyst. It has been shown that crisis is most likely to provide the catalyst for organization, such as was the case for the American G.I. Forum. The Forum was organized around an incident in Three Rivers, Texas—the refusal of military burial to a Mexican American war veteran in that community. This crisis orientation, this activation, must then probably be kept going; that is, institutionalized in some manner. One way to do this is to focus on a specific issue or problem, such as abuse by the police, and focus organizational activities towards resolving that issue. If successful, the organization can move on to other problem areas.

Leadership. This, of course, is very important to organizational viability, and every effort must be made to find leaders who have those qualities which can best help the organization to stick together and work toward its goals. The ideal leader would have a magnetic personality, attracting others to him, and would at the same time have some respect for the sensibilities of other persons. Leadership should probably be decentralized to combat the tendency towards elitism that exists in any organization.

Ethnic loyalty. Any successful Chicano organization should include a strong appeal to ethnic loyalty. That one consideration can overcome class, age, sex, and regional differences. Since ethnicity has in fact been a main consideration in the dominant society's relationships with the Chicano, often overriding all other factors, this seems a natural basis for organization. So the use of ethnic symbolism—flags, handshakes, slogans, language—would probably tend to promote organizational cohesion.

Needs of Chicano professionals. A final characteristic not mentioned by Tirado, but becoming increasingly important, is that some organizations should meet the specific needs of the newly emerging Chicano professional. Now that Chicanos are increasingly entering the professional ranks, there is a need for organizations which allow them to come together socially while pooling their talents and expertise. In this way they can contribute more meaningfully to the Chicano community.

Examples of these organizations include the Chicano Social Science Association, founded in 1973 at Highlands University in Las Vegas, New Mexico. Through this association Chicano social scientists across the nation meet, exchange views and information, and establish a network for both social and professional communication. Comparable groups exist at local levels, most commonly among Chicano educators.

Lower-class concerns. One final comment must be added regarding Chicano organizations. By and large, most of the groups described here have an overwhelmingly middle-class orientation. Since Mexican Americans are primarily working class, very few of them could have been involved with these groups. If organizations develop which include lower-class concerns, it is likely that Chicano organizational membership would increase dramatically within a very short period. To date, however, such organizations have not developed.

Conclusion

In sum, it can be said that Chicanos have not used ethnic organizations to the extent that they might have. The reasons used to explain this, however, vary depending on the model used to describe Chicano political experience. The elitist model would imply that any organizational activity that was allowed to exist would be inconsequential. Any organization that threatened the basic distribution of resources would be coopted or terminated.

The pluralistic model would assert that Chicanos could have developed organizations if they had so chosen. That more effective, broader organizations did not develop shows either that Chicanos had no need for ethnic organizations or that they were incapable of establishing them. Such an analysis, ignoring completely the history of Chicano organizational efforts, must be disregarded.

The internal colonial analysis, on the other hand, emphasizes the role oppression and violence have played in preventing Chicano organizational development. At the individual level, Chicanos are kept poor, uneducated, unemployed, and underemployed, preventing them from developing the interest or having the time to become involved in Chicano organizations. At the group level, organizations that are established are either destroyed, as is the case with Chicano labor groups; or they reinforce the system, as has LULAC; or they are harassed and kept minimally effective, as the G.I. Forum and MAPA have been. Those organizations that openly threaten the system are attacked and broken, as the Brown Berets have been.

Clearly, the internal colonial model seems more accurate, yet it is not completely satisfactory. For example, despite the regional differences that exist among Chicanos, it seems that politically conscious activists today should be at least able to agree on what to call themselves. Similarly, different age groups should be able to come together to fight common problems if they choose to do so. Perhaps the reasons for not overcoming these differences can be found in the legacy of colonialism, but at this writing it seems that many of the issues which prevent the formation of a united effort are relatively inconsequential. Failure to overcome them, therefore, is at least partially the result of petty jealousies and misunderstandings. While such internal conflicts are common to any mass-based effort, as is evidenced by the continuous battles waged within the Republican and Democratic parties, the Chicano movement will have great difficulty in achieving its major objectives if it does not first heal these internal divisions.

Chapter 6
Notes

1. See chapter 1 for a discussion of the role of groups in American society.
2. William V. D'Antonio and William H. Form, *Influentials in Two Border Cities: A Study in Community Decision-Making* (Notre Dame: University of Notre Dame Press, 1965).
3. Arthur J. Rubel, *Across the Tracks: Mexican Americans in a Texas City*, (Austin, Texas: University of Texas Press, 1966).
4. Miguel David Tirado, "Mexican American Community Political Organization: The Key to Chicano Political Power," *Aztlan* 1, no. 1 (Spring 1970): 53-78; Salvador Alvarez, "Mexican American Community Organizations," in *Voices: Readings from El Grito*, ed. Octavio I. Romano V. (Berkeley: Quinto Sol, 1971), pp. 91-101; Maurilio Vigil, "Ethnic Organizations Among the Mexican Americans of New Mexico: A Political Perspective" (Ph.D. dissertation, University of New Mexico, 1975).
5. For a discussion of ethnic group activities outside of the Southwest see Edgar Litt, *Ethnic Politics in America* (Glenview, Illinois: Scott, Foresman, 1970), pp. 42-59.
6. Mario Barrera, Carlos Muñoz, and Charles Ornelas, "The Barrio as an Internal Colony," in *People and Politics in Urban Society: Urban Affairs Annual Review*, vol. 6, ed. Harlan Hahn (Beverly Hills: Sage, 1972) p. 474.

7. Oral interview with Congressman Edward Roybal conducted by Oscar J. Martinez, Director, Institute of Oral History, University of Texas at El Paso, October 23, 1975, Transcript #195, p. 15.

8. Richard Santillan, *La Raza Unida* (Los Angeles: Tlaquilo Publications, 1973), pp. 36-38.

9. John Staples Shockley, *Chicano Revolt in a Texas Town* (Notre Dame: University of Notre Dame Press, 1974), pp. 24-41.

10. Special issue on "Labor History and the Chicano," *Aztlan* 6, no. 2 (Summer 1975). Coeditors for the special issue are Luis Leobardo Arroyo and Victor B. Nelson-Cisneros, both of the Department of History, UCLA.

11. Rodolfo Acuña; *Occupied America: The Chicano's Struggle for Liberation* (San Francisco: Canfield Press, 1972), pp. 153-186.

12. Raymond H. C. Teske, Jr. and Bardin H. Nelson, "Mexican American Political Power: A Dilemma" (paper presented at the Western Social Science Association, May 1975), pp. 8-9.

13. Biliana Ambrecht and Harry Pachon, "Ethnic Political Mobilization in a Mexican American Community: An Exploratory Study of East Los Angeles 1965-1972," *Western Political Quarterly* 28 (September 1974): 510.

14. Teske and Nelson, "Mexican American Political Power," p. 8.

15. F. Chris Garcia, "Political Miseducation for Mexican Americans," in *Ghosts in the Barrio: Issues in Bilingual Education*, ed. Ralph Poblano (San Rafael, Calif.: Leswing Press, 1973), pp. 143-148.

16. The point is explicitly made through comparisons in Maurilio Vigil, "Ethnic Organizations Among the Mexican Americans of New Mexico."

17. Sidney Verba and Norman Nie, *Participation in America: Political Democracy and Social Equality* (New York: Harper and Row, 1972), pp. 176-177.

18. Verba and Nie, *Participation in America*, pp. 202-208.

19. Frank L. Baird and Jesus F. Guzman, Jr., "Mexican Americans in Lubbock: Political Subculture and Mexican American Political Behavior" (paper presented at the Rocky Mountain Social Science Association Meeting, April 1973), p. 22.

20. There is in Washington, D.C. the National Congress of Hispanic American Citizens (El Congreso), but this is primarily a local Washington D.C. pressure group rather than a true association of allied regionally based organizations.

21. Tirado, "Mexican American Community Political Organizations."

Chicanos and the Electoral Process:

"Dar y quitar, pecado mortal."*

Elections and the two-party system stand as the pillars of the American political process. It is through elections that citizens are to exercise their influence and make their demands known, and it is the function of political parties to inform and mobilize citizens so that they can make their views heard and select their representatives. In principle, these two institutions, more than any others, serve to link the public with its leaders and to insure that the American people have a voice in shaping and controlling their future.[1]

Myth and Reality of Chicano Political Life

Traditional studies of Chicano political life, grounded in the belief in the effectiveness of the American electoral process, conclude that Chicanos' principal problem is their inability and unwillingness to utilize the political process properly. These observers of the political scene have assumed that since among ethnic minorities Chicanos have made the least use of elections to attain and exercise influence, Chicanos are ultimately responsible for their own lack of representation and attainments.

Although it is true that Chicanos have generally not been very active in traditional political life, there are some major exceptions to this generality. For example in New Mexico, where Chicano institutions predated and survived the United States takeover and Chicanos were in a majority, the electoral process has long been used successfully by the people. In this chapter we will further attempt to show that (1) in fact Chicanos have participated in electoral politics as long as they have been part of the United States, and (2) the real reasons that more Chicanos do not participate are a combination of factors, including primarily restrictions and prohibitions imposed upon Chicanos by the dominant society, not any inherent cultural trait.

*To give and then to take away is a mortal sin."

Perhaps one of the most important characteristics of Chicano electoral behavior is that some Chicanos have long demonstrated a faith in the importance of the electoral process. Historically this faith has been shown through the Mexican community's continued efforts to win office.[2] More recently, a study in California and Texas documented the depth of commitment Chicanos have to the political process; 80 percent of the Texas sample and 81 percent of the Los Angeles sample agreed that "voting decides what happens."[3] Such a high level of support might in fact be interpreted as unrealistic.

Patterns of Registration and Voting

Despite this apparent belief in elections, it is well documented that, except in New Mexico, Mexican Americans vote less than Anglo Americans and often less than blacks as well. Voting, however, must be conceived as a two-step process—citizens must first register and then they must vote. Analyzing Chicano electoral behavior at each of these levels lends great insight into Chicano political life. Table 7-1 presents data describing Chicano voter registration.

Registration

The data suggest several patterns. First, Chicanos register to vote at levels comparable to and often higher than Anglos in Texas. In fact, between 1960 and 1970, Anglos outregistered Chicanos only once. It is also significant that in Los Angeles Chicanos register at rates comparable to those of Texas Chicanos, yet Anglos greatly outregister them. The third item evidenced in Table 7-1 is that Chicanos are not registering to vote in particularly high numbers, although the trend in Texas suggests that registration is regularly increasing. In New Mexico, Chicanos in the northern "Hispanic" counties (Mexican American population 60 percent or greater) are registered at a rate greater than Anglos in that area and at least equal to that of Anglos in other parts of the state. But in areas of the state in which Chicanos are more recent residents and are in a minority of the population, their registration rates lag behind those of the Anglo majority.

Data from Colorado and Arizona support the California example. In Tucson, Arizona, Mexican American precincts average 13 percent lower registration than Anglo precincts,[4] and in Denver comparable Anglo precincts average over 20 percent higher registration than Chi-

Table 7-1
Chicano Voter Registration as a Percent of Eligible Chicano Population

	Los Angeles[b]		*San Antonio*		*Texas*[a]	
	Mex. Am.	*Anglo*	*Mex. Am.*	*Anglo*	*Mex. Am.*	*All*
1960					46	47
1962					44	43
1964	56	77	46	43	52	51
1966					53	48
1968					65	64
1970			47[c]	62	70	63

[a] Clifton McCleskey and Bruce Merrill, "Mexican American Political Behavior in Texas," *Social Science Quarterly* 53, no. 4 (March 1973), p. 787. Includes all Texas data.

[b]1964 Los Angeles and San Antonio data from Grebler et al., *Mexican American People*, pp. 563-567.

[c]1970 San Antonio data from Andy Hernandez, Trinity University, unpublished paper, 1974. Data applies to all precincts 70 percent Anglo or Spanish surnamed.

cano precincts.[5] Nationwide statistics further indicate that Chicanos are greatly underregistered in comparison to Anglos and even in comparison to blacks. While 73 percent of the Anglo and 68 percent of the black populations are registered, only 44 percent of the Spanish-surnamed people are registered.[6]

Voting

The differences between Chicano and Anglo voting behavior are even greater than the differences in registration. Data from across the Southwest indicate similar patterns. In Los Angeles in 1969 during the race for mayor, Chicano precincts turned out at 16 percent lower levels than did the typical city precinct.[7] In Denver Chicano precincts turned out at 19 percent lower levels.[8] Nationwide, 38 percent of registered Spanish-surnamed citizens voted, while 65 percent and 54 percent, respectively, of the white and black registered populations voted.[9] The exception is New Mexico, where the Hispanic areas of the state turned out at a 70.3 percent rate for the 1974 general election, compared to a statewide turnout of 65.1 percent and a national average of 40.7 percent.[10]

Chicanos thus are generally not using the ballot. At a time when black voters in the South were making great strides toward equality at the ballot box, Spanish Americans, both Chicanos and Puerto Ricans, were voting less.[11] In 1964, 15 percent fewer Chicanos voted than in 1960, and in 1968 almost one-third fewer voted in Arizona and Colorado, and almost 17 percent less in California.[12]

Table 7-2
Chicano Voters as a Percent of Registered Chicanos

	Los Angeles		*San Antonio*		*Texas*[a]	
	Mex. Am.	*Anglo*	*Mex. Am.*	*Anglo*	*Mex. Am.*	*All*
1960					79[b]	89
1962					65	64
1964	50[b]	60	38	60	76	87
1966					41	48
1968					61	76
1970					48	54

[a]McCleskey and Merrill, "Mexican American Political Behavior in Texas," p. 787.
[b]Grebler et al., *The Mexican American People,* pp. 563-567.

Reasons for Nonparticipation

Why do Chicanos register less than Anglos? Why, if Chicanos register to vote, do they not vote? These are the questions which we must answer before determining which model can best be used to explain Chicano participation in electoral politics.

Deliberate Obstacles

Perhaps the most important single answer is that many obstacles have been placed in the way of Chicanos' exercising their electoral rights.[13] There are many examples of Chicanos being intimidated, threatened, and even physically abused as they have attempted to exercise their constitutional right to the franchise. Representatives of the power structure have threatened Chicanos with retaliation, such as loss of employment or loss of government services such as welfare pensions or food stamps, if they attempt to vote.[14] Until recently several states have had literacy tests which require proficiency in the reading and writing of the English language—a requirement which, of course, discriminates against non-English-speaking citizens. Literacy tests as a requirement for voting have very recently been abolished. For example, in California a 1970 state supreme court decision declared that Spanish literacy was sufficient for voting qualification.[15]

Residency laws also worked particular hardships on both recent immigrants from Mexico and substantial groups of Chicano migrants, who either follow the crops or move from one urban industrial area to another seeking a decent level of employment. Several methods, ostensibly operating within the law, have actually bent it to prohibit Chicanos from registering and voting. For example, in many areas, such as in South Texas, registration has been held at only one centralized location, usually the county courthouse. Chicanos had to make an extra effort to go to the central location, even though they usually feel quite ill at ease in governmental office buildings.

Also, time schedules for registering are usually manipulated in order to make registration very inconvenient for Chicanos. Until recently the requirements in Texas were that voting registration locations were open only on week days between 8 AM and 5 PM. This requirement worked a particular hardship on the Chicano community, since these areas are overwhelmingly Chicano and since Chicanos are overwhelmingly members of the working class. In other words, Chicanos as a population suffered more because of these restrictions than did Anglos. Registration was also required during the time of the year in which Chicanos were generally on the migrant trail, absent from their southern Texas homes. Texas also used a "non-permanent" registration, requiring that all voters must reregister each year in order to maintain their voting eligibility.

Felony Laws

Most states still disenfranchise persons convicted of felonies. The fact that Chicanos are found in disproportionately high numbers among inmates of penitentiaries means that they are also disproportionately disenfranchised. In hearings before the California State Advisory Committee to the U.S. Commission on Civil Rights, Sacramento attorney John Moulds elaborated upon this situation in California:

> There are approximately 40,000 adult inmates and parolees in the California Adult Authority Corrections System. Of these, 20 percent or 8,000 are from the Southern California area . . . . Most Mexican American convictions are for narcotics offenses. Because of the numerous, interrelated institutional discriminatory practices that result in more poor Mexican Americans being arrested, convicted and imprisoned for narcotic offenses than middle class persons, their punishment is made even more severe because they lose their right to vote, they become politically helpless to participate in the American democratic process to change those social conditions that caused their initial downfall, and which will also cause their future downfall.[16]

Permanent Aliens

In areas of the Southwest close to the Mexican border an additional problem is that there are a great many permanent aliens who are disfranchised because they cannot qualify to become citizens of the United States. The main reason they cannot qualify is usually that they lack an adequate facility with the English language. Thus, citizenship tests which require literacy in English prevent permanent residents, who in every other manner share the obligations and duties of residents of the United States, from exercising their electoral rights.

Low Socioeconomic Status

Compounding all of these problems is the fact that most Chicanos possess those socioeconomic characteristics which are most associated with low levels of political activity. These include low formal education, low income and occupational level, and a rural background. Significantly, those Mexican Americans in California who stated that "voting decides what happens" also stated that politics is too complicated to understand. While they agree they should vote, they are implicitly admitting that they do not have the information they need to vote effectively.[17]

Their behavior in Texas and elsewhere reflects this lack of information. In Denver in 1972, only 23 percent of Chicano respondents could correctly identify members of the city council, while 41 percent of the Anglo and 29 percent of the black populations were able to correctly identify these officials.[18] While 61 percent of the Anglos and 52 percent of the blacks follow public affairs "most of the time," only 42 percent of the Chicano community does so.[19] In Texas, Chicanos are much less likely to discuss politics with their friends than are either Anglos or blacks.[20]

The Unresponsive System

Surely a major reason for this disinterest is that Chicanos do not believe that the system has responded to them even when they have participated. When asked if "people like themselves have a great deal to say about government," 35 percent of Los Angeles Chicano respondents and 40 percent of those in San Antonio said no. More importantly, 44 percent of Los Angelenos and 47 percent of San Antonio Chicanos did not agree that public officials care about their constituents.[21] Chicano residents of Denver display comparable dissatisfaction. Only 33 percent of them believe they are getting their tax dollar's worth of benefits, compared with 63 percent of the Anglo population.[22] Only 4 percent of the Chicanos in Denver have a "positive" reaction to city officials, compared to 11 percent positive reaction among Anglos.[23]

Ties to Mexico

Some observers have also stated that because of this exclusion from the system and their close ties to Mexico, many Chicanos feel more attached to Mexico than to the United States. Armando Rendon, for example, states that one reason that Chicanos do not participate to the extent that one might expect is that they cling to the dream, actually a myth, that their stay in the United States is a temporary one. When they have improved their condition, they say, they will return to their native land of Mexico. Thus, feeling that they are only temporary residents of the United States and not part of this system, they are consequently less likely to participate in the politics of the United States.[24]

Ralph Guzman explains the view that some Mexicans may have of their relationship to political participation in the United States system:

> In terms of themselves, that is the Mexican American people, their political efficiency was remarkable; they were able to ignore the American political system and still survive as a people. They turned away from citizen naturalization and voter registration consciously and deliberately. They said, in effect, as no other immigrant group had done, "we do not need you, we do not want you, go away, mister." This refusal to join, to play gringo politics, meant that their neighborhoods were left without curbs, sidewalks, streetlights and other governmental services. Many Mexican Americans seemed to prefer barrios that were comfortable, close replicas of villages in the homeland.[25]

Discrepancy between Registration and Voting

As a result of all these factors, many Mexican Americans have been estranged from the political process. On the one hand, they register to vote because in some cases it is relatively easy to do so and sometimes difficult to avoid. Registration drives make registration a passive act—all you need to do is stay at home, and a registrar will find you. Furthermore, these registrars are Spanish speaking, and registering thus requires no psychological price or embarrassment. Voting, however, requires time, information and an explicit commitment to act. Because of factors described throughout this book, Chicanos are increasingly unwilling to make this commitment.

Chicano Voting Behavior

Whether or not Chicanos exercise their voting power, they are in a position to play an important role in politics from the local to the national level.

Potential Voting Power

They are concentrated in certain geographical areas in the Southwest and constitute substantial minorities as well as majorities in cities and congressional districts throughout the area. As of 1973, the Spanish-speaking voting age population in twenty-six congressional districts in Arizona, California, Colorado, New Mexico, and Texas was larger than the victory margin in these districts.[26] Chicanos, in other words, are in a position to determine the outcome of elections in these districts.

This potential for influence and power is also evident in other parts of the country such as in the Chicago-Gary, Indiana area, where approximately 400,000 Chicanos reside. Overall, fifty of seventy-eight southwestern congressional districts have a Chicano population of at least 10 percent, and six of these have Chicano populations of 47 percent of more.[27] Nationwide, thirty-nine congressional districts have Spanish-surnamed populations ranging from 15 to 75 percent, all but five of these in the Southwest.[28] The future potential of Chicano electoral power is even greater, since the median age of Chicanos is under 18, while the national median age is almost 30.

Despite these numbers, Chicanos have not exercised their franchise as effectively as might have been expected. In analyzing Chicano voting behavior it is most useful to examine voting patterns at the national, state, and local levels.

Presidential Voting Patterns

The 1960 election. In 1960 Chicanos showed the nation and especially the Democratic Party that their vote was indeed significant. The close race between John F. Kennedy and Richard Nixon gave Chicanos their maximum opportunity to act as a balance of power factor. In some key areas Chicanos gave Kennedy just enough votes to enable him to carry several states. In that election year, the Democrats made strenuous efforts to insure Chicano support for their party. The Democrats were at a disadvantage in that they were running a relatively unknown junior senator from Massachusetts against a vice president who had served under a very popular Republican president, Dwight D. Eisenhower. Eisenhower had been a great vote-getter among Democrats, including Chicanos.

The uncertainty of the Democrats motivated them to attempt to mobilize the Chicano community. John Kennedy became an honorary member of LULAC. "Viva Kennedy" clubs were formed throughout the Southwest, and voter registration and education drives were consequently in full swing. That Kennedy and the Democrats succeeded in their efforts is illustrated by the following voting statistics, as well as by the fact that the Kennedy family, particularly John, won the hearts of Chicano people. Pictures of the martyred president and his brother RFK are still found in homes of Chicanos throughout the Southwest, often alongside their little home altars.

Chicanos responded to the Democratic effort and John F. Kennedy by giving him an 85 percent vote nationwide. The Chicano vote was vital for Kennedy in New Mexico and Texas where he did not receive a majority of the Anglo vote. In New Mexico, Kennedy garnered 70 percent of the Chicano vote, giving him a 20,000-vote plurality. This was significant in light of the fact that he only carried New Mexico by a 2,000 vote margin. In Texas he received an even more substantial 91 percent of the Chicano vote, or a whopping 200,000 plurality. This again was the difference in winning the state's electoral vote, since JFK carried the state of Texas by only 50,000 votes. In the other three southwestern states of Colorado, Arizona, and California, Kennedy won at least 75 percent of the Chicano vote, but not enough Chicanos had registered and voted to tip the balance in Kennedy's favor in these states. But the election revealed the kind of impact that Chicanos can have in highly contested elections, even those at the national level.

The election of 1964. This election revealed a potential weakness in Chicano voting influence, since it was characterized by a disappointingly low turnout. With Kennedy's assassination, Chicanos' interest in and excitement about American politics diminished. Furthermore, the 1964 race gave them a choice between a person who had voted against the Civil Rights Act of 1964 and a Texan who had exhibited at best a paternalistic attitude towards Chicanos. The Democratic candidate, Lyndon Johnson, did win 90 percent of the Chicano vote and carried all the Southwestern states except his opponent's home state of Arizona. But the voting turnout dropped substantially. In some Chicano precincts in New Mexico, for example, nearly 15 percent fewer voters turned out in 1964 than in 1960. One of the main reasons that Goldwater carried his own state was that in Arizona Chicano voting turnout was down by as much as one-third, which took votes away from the Democrats.

The 1968 election. In 1968 the Chicano electorate continued to shrink, although the percentage of votes for the Democrats continued high. Hubert Humphrey received 87 percent of the Chicano vote while his Republican opponent, Richard Nixon, received only 10 percent. Again, Chicano turnout was down by as much as one-third in some precincts in Arizona and Colorado. Even though Hubert Humphrey won six of every seven votes cast by Chicanos in California, the turnout was down by one-sixth compared to the 1960 level of participation. Among the factors producing a reduced turnout was the fact that many Chicanos had supported Robert Kennedy in his bid for the Democratic nomination; his murder had a particularly disheartening effect on the Chicano political community.

The Texas pattern seemed to be an exception, as several factors there led to an increase in Chicano participation. The poll tax was abolished in 1966. Labor unions, such as the AFL-CIO and other liberal groups, engaged in massive registration drives in Texas and registered many thousands of Chicanos. Consequently the turnout rose by more than 20 percent from the 1960 level, and most of these votes were Democratic, as Humphrey received an impressive 93 percent of the Chicano vote. This almost unanimous support gave Humphrey a margin of 300,000 votes over Nixon in the Chicano areas of Texas. This was particularly important since Humphrey carried Texas by only 39,000 votes.

Although Nixon's overall Chicano support fell five percentage points from 1968 to 1972, he did make one noticeable gain. In New Mexico, Nixon won almost four out of every ten votes cast in Chicano precincts. Nixon's inroads into the Chicano vote helped him carry the state, as Humphrey came out of Chicano precincts in New

Mexico leading Nixon by only 10,000. Nixon quickly overcame this margin in the Anglo precincts of populous Albuquerque.

The 1972 election. This election revealed an increasing sophistication among Chicano voters. Chicanos seemed to be using the vote more to reward their friends and punish their enemies, as any group bidding for political influence must do. The increased Chicano political consciousness and awareness of the unique status of the Chicano, the rise of La Raza Unida Party, and increasing criticisms of the two major political parties as irrelevant to the Chicano's needs—all resulted in a diminished electoral turnout and lower levels of support for the Democratic party.

Nationwide, Chicanos voted about two to one for the Democratic party. The vote was almost two to one for Democrat George McGovern over Richard Nixon—thirty-six percent for Nixon, 64 percent for McGovern. This was the lowest level of Chicano support for a presidential candidate in many years. However, it should be remembered that Richard Nixon won one of the most sweeping victories in the history of American presidential elections and that the percentage of Chicano votes for Nixon was much lower than his nationwide electoral margin.

Nixon won his strongest Chicano vote in New Mexico, where three out of every seven Chicanos voted for him—a 43 percent increase in Republican support over 1968. In California, the Chicano vote for Nixon doubled from four years earlier as the Chicano Republican percentage jumped from 12 percent to 26 percent. But in Texas the situation was quite different as the Chicano third party, La Raza Unida, made its presence felt. LRUP did not endorse the presidential candidate of either major party. Its leaders had offered their support for George McGovern if he, in turn, would endorse the party's state-wide candidates over their Democratic opponents. McGovern, however, did not accept their offer. He did not endorse Raza Unida candidates, and thus Raza Unida did not endorse him.

Nixon won 20 percent of the Chicano vote, which was an increase of some 14 percent from 1968. But La Raza Unida did run candidates for senator and governor, and their candidate for governor, Ramsey Muniz, won fully one-third (over 200,000 votes, 6 percent of the total) of the Chicano vote. This achievement cut down the margin of victory in this predominantly one-party Democratic state to 61 percent for the Democratic candidate, Dolph Briscoe. Briscoe came out of Chicano precincts with only a 55 percent plurality.

Congressional Voting Patterns

Chicano voting at congressional and state levels also reveals certain patterns, but important variations exist from region to region.

Support of Democrats. Most significantly, Chicanos have been overwhelmingly supportive of Democratic congressional and senatorial candidates throughout the Southwest. In 1960, 86 percent of Chicano voters supported Democratic congressional candidates throughout the Southwest; in 1964, this figure was 87 percent; in 1968, 85 percent, and in 1972, even with the Nixon inroads, the figure remained at 85 percent. In 1975, therefore, it was not surprising that three of four Chicano congressmen were Democrats: Eligio de la Garza of Corpus Christi, Texas; Henry B. González of San Antonio; and Edward R. Roybal of Los Angeles. Manuel Lujan, Jr. of Albuquerque is the only Republican.

Senatorial races. Chicano senatorial candidates are extremely rare, and only New Mexico has produced Chicano senators. Chicano voters have been crucial in electing Joseph Montoya, the New Mexico Democrat, and he is keenly aware of the increasing sophistication and independence of Chicano voters. In 1964, when Montoya first won his senate seat, he defeated his Republican opponent Ed Mechem by 31,000 votes, with 74 percent Chicano support. Six years later, in the 1970 senatorial election, Montoya, with the advantage of incumbency, was running against a conservative Republican, Anderson Carter. Montoya expected an easy win under these circumstances; registered Democrats in New Mexico outnumber Republicans two and a half to one, and Montoya had strong support from unions and other liberal groups.

Montoya won, but this time by only 16,000 votes. The Chicano voter again made the difference, for the turnout in Chicano precincts was strong. Montoya won 77 percent of this Chicano vote; Anderson Carter, 21 percent. Montoya's 77 percent gave him a plurality of 25,000 votes in the Chicano areas. This margin was necessary for victory, since the senator won only 47 percent of the Anglo vote statewide. Thus, the statewide victory margin of 16,000 came from his own people. This illustrates well the importance of the Chicano vote in determining the electoral fortunes of Chicano politicians.

State-Level Voting Patterns

With the exception of some instances in New Mexico, Chicanos had not run for state-wide offices until 1970.

Contests for governor. In that year, Democrat Raul Castro sought and won the Democratic nomination for governor in Arizona against the efforts of party stalwarts. Despite his political conservatism, Castro mobilized Chicanos because of his Mexican ancestry. He won 90 percent of the Chicano vote, but this tremendous support was not sufficient to carry the election for him because of a relatively low turnout in Chicano precincts. Thus the incumbent Republican governor was reelected.

The low turnout among Chicanos was the result of a number of factors, including a decision by the Republican-dominated legislature to cleanse the voting rolls and have all citizens reregister. This cleansing of the rolls erased the results of years of registration drives in barrios across the state. It seems certain that many Chicanos did not understand that they had to reregister, were confused by this development, and simply stayed away from the polls.

In 1974, Castro again won the Democratic nomination, this time with the support of the party leaders. He went on to win the election and become Arizona's first Mexican American governor. 1974 also saw Jerry Apodaca elected governor of New Mexico in a hotly contested race. Like Governor Castro, Apodaca is a Democrat and owes his election to the support of the Chicano community.[29] Thus, although there are not many examples of Chicano voting patterns at the state level, those that are available indicate that Chicano voters support Chicano candidates, and that Chicano candidates run as Democrats.

State legislature elections: California. Chicano electoral success has been greatest at district and local levels where the sheer force of numbers can not be denied, or at least is much more difficult to repress. Nonetheless, in California, political structures have been successful in minimizing Chicano representation. Since 1848, Chicanos have always been underrepresented in the state assembly and senate, and often there have been no Chicanos in either chamber.[30]

From 1849 to 1973 over 900 individuals served in the senate and over 3075 in the state assembly. During this time only 9 Chicanos were elected to the senate and 24 to the assembly, and half of these 33 were elected between 1849 and 1864. In 1974, the first Chicano in sixty-two years won election to the state senate, and Chicanos made noteworthy gains in the state assembly as well. This general lack of representation is not related to a lack of candidates. Between 1960 and 1970 alone, 11 Chicanos ran unsuccessfully for the state senate, and 56 ran for the assembly.

It is significant that Chicano candidates tend to represent heavily Chicano districts. Twenty-one of twenty-four Chicano assemblymen in California have been elected from these areas. These districts are so defined, however, that they can not be considered "safe"; that is, there is not a substantial Chicano majority. Thus few Chicanos are re-elected often enough to develop the seniority necessary to become influential with the assembly.

State legislature elections: Colorado. Chicanos in Colorado have enjoyed more electoral success than their *carnales* (brothers) in California, but overall they have had little impact on policy.[31] A major reason for Chicanos attaining office in Colorado is that until 1952 Chicanos were highly concentrated in southern Colorado, and the sheer force of numbers enabled them to win elections in these districts. Despite their concentrated numbers, however, Chicanos have elected only five state senators. A shift in the Chicano population has greatly affected representational patterns. Prior to 1952 all Chicano state officials were elected in southern Colorado; since then, of the fourteen Chicanos to win state office, twelve have been elected from other areas, including Denver.

Except for one ten-year period, including territorial days, Chicanos have always been represented in either one or both legislative chambers. But as in California, few of these representatives were able to develop seniority. Overall the Chicano population has been greatly underrepresented in the house and senate throughout the history of the state. Nonetheless, there is no question that Chicanos have had much more success in state-level electoral politics in Colorado than in California. As of 1974, for example, the Speaker of the House was Ruben Valdez, a Chicano who is an open and aggressive advocate of Chicano issues.

State legislature elections: New Mexico. The Chicano experience in New Mexico differs completely from that in any other state. "Chicanos have at one time or another held virtually every type of position in state and local government. Chicanos are recognized as a potent political force which must be dealt with. Practices which have the effect of diluting the Chicano vote, such as racial gerrymandering and literacy requirements, appear to have been negligible if they existed at all."[32]

Since 1912 New Mexico has had three Chicano governors, including the incumbent Jerry Apodaca, seven lieutenant governors, including Roberto Mondragón who served until 1974, eight secretaries of state, and numerous other officers elected statewide. Chicanos have been well represented in the state legislature. Three times they have held a majority; on several occasions Chicanos have served as president of the senate and Speaker of the House. Only in the judiciary have Chicanos been underrepresented, but even there they have enjoyed comparatively substantial representation.

State legislature elections: Arizona. The pattern of representation in Arizona resembles that of Colorado. In those districts where there is a heavy Chicano concentration there has been somewhat regular Chicano representation. Thus Pima County in southern Arizona has long sent Chicanos to both the state house and senate. Because these are "safe districts," Chicanos have been able to develop seniority and attain positions of influence within their respective chambers. The present senate majority leader, for example, is a young, active and outspoken Chicano. Overall, however, Chicanos in Arizona have been greatly underrepresented in both the house and senate.

State legislature elections:Texas. The Texas example more closely parallels the Californian experience. A primary difference between the two is that in Texas violence has been a more common means of disenfranchising voters. Whatever the means, despite highly concentrated Chicano populations Chicanos have a very disproportionately small representation in the Texas legislature.

Overall, then, the pattern is clear. With the exception of New Mexico, Chicanos, despite their numbers and concentration, are unable to elect their own representatives. Table 7-3 illustrates how, in every state in the Southwest, Chicanos are significantly underrepresented in their respective state legislatures.

This pattern of exclusion in the legislature is made worse by similar patterns in other state-wide decision-making bodies. State boards of education, for example, exclude Chicanos to a comparable extent as Table 7-4 illustrates.

Table 7-3
Chicano Representation in State Legislatures[a]

State	*Total Number of Legislators*	*Number of Chicano Legislators*	*Chicano Percent of Total Legislators*	*Chicano Percent of Total Population*
Arizona	90	11	11.1 percent	18.8 percent
California	118	5	4.2	15.5
Colorado	100	4	4.0	13.0
New Mexico	112	32	34.0	40.1
Texas	181	10	5.5	18.4

[a]As of March 1973.

Table 7-4
Mexican American Representation on State Boards of Education[a]

State	Number of Mexican Americans	Total Number Board Members	Mexican American Percent of Total Board Members	Percent of Mexican American Students
Arizona	0	9	0	19.5
California	1	10	10	16.5
Colorado	0	5	0	13.7
New Mexico	3	10	30	39.4
Texas	2	24	8.3	22.6

[a]U.S. Commission on Civil Rights, *Toward Quality Education for Mexican Americans, Report 6, Mexican American Education Study,* February 1974, p. 13.

Local Voting Patterns

It is surprising that even at local levels, where concentration of Chicanos should be most likely to make their influence felt, similar and even more exaggerated patterns of exclusion exist. Data on representation at local levels have not been compiled for the entire southwestern area, but the information that does exist documents the extent to which Chicanos are kept from holding even local office.

Tucson elections. In Tucson, Arizona no Chicano was elected to the city council for decades. Over one twenty-five year period from 1945 to 1969, 111 candidates ran for these offices, but only 5 Chicanos were among these candidates. Since World War II, there has been no Chicano mayoral candidate.[33]

Recently, however, Chicanos in Tucson have organized themselves and have begun to elect their own councilmen. Currently, there are two Chicanos serving in that capacity. It is noteworthy, however, that the first Chicano to win a position on the city council since the 1940s did so only after Raza Unida ran its own candidate. Apparently Democratic party leaders were unwilling to risk the loss of Chicano voters to Raza Unida and thus jeopardize their overall electoral chances, so they nominated a Chicano and mobilized party support to insure his election. By combining party support and Chicano votes, the Chicano candidate's election was assured.

Texas local elections. In Texas, Chicanos are notoriously underrepresented in city council positions, as Table 7-5 documents. This exclusion has permeated all of Texas politics, even those areas in South Texas that are almost completely Chicano. It was only with the advent of Raza Unida in Crystal City, (see p. 170) that this pattern began to be broken.[34] Today Chicanos are benefitting from increasing representation in these areas, but they are still underrepresented throughout the state.

California systematically excludes Chicanos from holding local offices, as they are excluded from federal and state offices. As of 1970, Chicanos held only 2.2 percent of all 10,907 city and county government positions in that state.[35] In Los Angeles, where approximately one million Chicanos reside, no Chicano has served on the city council since Edward Roybal held that position in the mid-1950s. In some areas, however, Chicanos have been able to overcome the obstacles of the system and gain political power. The best example of this is Parlier City where, in Crystal City-like fashion, Chicanos have completely taken over the city (see p. 176).[36]

The question of effectiveness. Although in many communities Chicanos have been elected to municipal. office, when examining these positions we must bear in mind that even having such a representative may be meaningless. For example, one Chicano on a city council of seven members is unlikely to have a great impact. In many such cases, Chicanos serve only symbolic roles. That is, they serve as symbols demonstrating the openness of the system and as role models for the Chicano community. Their policy impact is usually minimal, however.

Only in the local governments of New Mexico does the proportion of local elected officials come close to the Chicano population.

Overall, then, there is no question that Chicanos are systematically underrepresented in elected offices at every level.

Table 7-5
Chicano Representation in City Councils in Selected Texas Cities, 1970[a]

City	*Percent of Mexican American Population*	*Percent of Mexican American City Councilmen*
Austin	16	0
Beaumont	4.5	0
Corpus Christi	40.5	14.3
Dallas	6.7	1.3
El Paso	58.1	11.4
Ft. Worth	9.2	0
Lubbock	16.0	0
San Antonio	52.1	27.0
Waco	7.4	0

[a]Charles L. Cotrell, "The Effects of At-Large Elections on the Political Access and Voting Strength of Mexican Americans" (paper presented at the Rocky Mountain Social Science Association Meeting, April 1974), p. 60.

Table 7-6
Mexican American Representation in New Mexico Counties

County	*1970 Population*[a]	*Spanish-Surnamed Population*[b]
Bernalillo	315,774	123,814 (39.2 percent)
Catron	2,202	927 (42.1)
Chavez	43,331	12,107 (27.9)
Colfax	12,170	6,464 (53.1)
Curry	39,517	6,872 (17.4)
DeBaca	2,547	1,039 (40.8)
Dona Ana	69,773	35,439 (50.8)
Eddy	41,119	12,555 (30.5)
Grant	22,030	12,354 (56.1)
Guadalupe	4,969	4,199 (84.5)
Harding	1,348	644 (49.3)
Hidalgo	4,908	2,784 (56.7)
Lea	49,554	6,202 (12.5)
Lincoln	7,560	2,568 (34.0)
Los Alamos	15,198	2,699 (17.8)
Luna	11,706	5,441 (46.5)
McKinley	43,208	8,626 (20.0)
Mora	4,673	4,419 (96.4)
Otero	41,097	9,730 (23.7)
Quay	10,903	3,924 (36.0)
Rio Arriba	25,170	20,691 (82.2)
Roosevelt	16,479	2,524 (15.3)
Sandoval	17,492	11,159 (63.8)
San Juan	52,515	6,903 (13.1)
San Miguel	21,951	17,943 (81.7)
Santa Fe	53,756	34,883 (65.0)
Sierra	7,189	2,577 (35.8)
Socorro	9,763	5,858 (60.0)
Taos	17,516	15,109 (86.3)
Torrance	5,290	2,783 (52.6)
Union	4,925	1,395 (28.3)
Valencia	40,539	22,634 (55.8)
STATE	1,016,172	407,286 (40.1)

Source: Compiled and calculated from: New Mexico Secretary of State's Office, *Roster of State of New Mexico, Elective State, Legislative and County Officials.*

[a]U.S. Department of Commerce, Bureau of the Census, *United States Census of Population: 1970*, vol. 1, *Characteristics of the Population*, pt. 33, New Mexico, p. 200.

[b]Ibid., pp. 222-224.

Bureaucratic Representation

This underrepresentation in elected offices is worsened by the fact that Chicanos are equally underrepresented in bureaucratic positions, and it is the bureaucracy which "is likely, day in and day out, to be our main source of policy initiative."[37]

Table 7-6 *(Continued)*

Elected County Officials	*Spanish-Surnamed Elected County Officials*	*Representation Differential (percent)*
16	3 (18.6 percent)	–20.6
10	2 (20.0)	–22.1
11	0 (0.0)	–27.9
10	2 (20.0)	–33.1
10	0 (0.0)	–17.4
9	1 (11.1)	–29.7
11	6 (54.5)	+ 3.7
11	0 (0.0)	–30.5
10	3 (30.0)	–26.1
10	10 (100.0)	+15.5
9	3 (33.3)	–23.2
9	3 (33.3)	–23.4
13	0 (0.0)	–12.5
11	4 (36.4)	+ 2.4
12	1 (8.3)	– 9.5
9	0 (0.0)	–46.5
11	3 (27.2)	+ 7.2[c]
9	8 (88.9)	– 5.7
11	1 (9.1)	–14.6
10	0 (0.0)	–36.0
10	10 (100.0)	+17.8
9	0 (0.0)	–15.3
10	7 (70.0)	+ 6.2[c]
10	0 (0.0)	–13.1[c]
10	9 (90.0)	+ 8.3
11	10 (90.9)	+25.9
9	2 (22.2)	–13.6
9	5 (55.6)	– 4.4
12	12 (100.0)	+13.7
10	3 (30.0)	–22.6
9	1 (11.1)	–17.2
12	9 (75.0)	+19.2
333	118 (35.4)	– 4.7

[c]Difficult to obtain accurate figures for Mexican-American population because of large numbers of Native Americans (American Indians).

Extent of Underrepresentation

The extent to which this underrepresentation exists throughout the national and state political systems is illustrated by the Californian experience as of 1970:

1. Of 15,650 elected and appointed officials at municipal, county, state, and federal levels, only 1.98 percent were Mexican American.

2. None of the 40 top state officials was Mexican American.

Table 7-7
Mexican American Representation in
New Mexico Municipalities

	Population		Spanish-Surname Population						
Municipalities	*1970*[a]	*1970*[b]	*1907*[a]	*1974*[b]	*Percent*	*Municipal*[c] *Officials*	*Spanish-Surname*[c] *Officials*	*Percent*	*Representation Differential (percent)*
Alamogordo	23,035	23,500	5,479	5,593	(23.8)	24	1	4.2	−19.6
Albuquerque	243,751	286,300	85,032	99,919	(34.9)	52	10	19.2	−15.7
Artesia	10,291	10,000	3,196	3,110	(31.1)	25	1	4.0	−27.1
Carlsbad	21,297	22,100	5,462	5,658	(25.6)	26	1	3.9	−21.7
Clovis	28,574	31,800	5,593	6,233	(19.6)	24	1	4.2	−15.4
Farmington	21,979	25,300	3,148	3,618	(14.3)	26	0	0.0	−14.3
Gallup	14,596	15,300	5,989	6,273	(41.0)	31	13	41.9	+ 0.9
Hobbs	26,169	26,200	2,942	2,934	(11.2)	26	1	3.8	− 7.4
Las Cruces	37,857	38,500	17,477	17,787	(46.2)	28	9	32.1	−14.1
Los Alamos	11,310	16,000	2,202	3,120	(19.5)	28	2	7.1	−12.4
Las Vegas	13,835	15,900	11,182	12,847	(80.8)	21	14	66.7	−14.1
Portales	10,554	10,600	2,119	2,131	(20.1)	21	1	4.8	−15.3
Roswell	33,908	37,100	8,196	8,978	(24.2)	27	0	0.0	−24.2
Santa Fe	41,167	43,100	26,641	27,886	(64.7)	27	13	48.1	−16.6
TOTAL	538,323	601,700	184,658	206,087	(34.3)	386	67	17.4	−16.9
Municipalities 2500-10,000	88,568	N/A	39,068	N/A	(44.1)	317	106	33.4	−10.7
Unincorporated 2500-10,000+	76,900	N/A	31,893	N/A		N/A			
Places>2,500	104,329	N/A	N/A	N/A		764	261	34.2	
	808,120					1,081	367	34.0	

[a]1970, *U.S. Census* (The official census figures are used in the percentage calculations).
[b]1974 Estimates, Bureau of Business Research, University of New Mexico.
[c]*1974 Directory of Municipal Officials of New Mexico.*

3. None of the top advisors to the governor was Mexican American.

4. Only 1.5 percent of the 4,023 positions in the executive branch, including boards and commissions, were filled by Mexican Americans.

5. Of all city and county officials 2.2 percent were Mexican American.

6. None of the 132 top state court positions, including supreme court justices, the Judicial Council, the Administrative Office of the Courts, the Commission on Judicial Qualification, and the State Court of Appeals, was held by a Mexican American.

7. Only 1.33 percent of federal officials, including legislators, marshals, United States attorneys, and their assistants, were Mexican American.

8. Only 6 Mexican Americans worked with the U.S. Court of Appeals and U.S. District Courts, including all judges, referees, probation officers, commissioners, and marshals. None of these 6 were judges or referees.

9. Only 7 of 700 state senate and assembly staff members listed in the official directory had Spanish surnames.[38]

When evaluating the significance and effectiveness of this exclusion, it is useful to recall that, except for New Mexico, California is reputed to be the state offering the greatest current opportunities to Chicanos.

Even in New Mexico, Chicanos are not proportionately represented in the top-echelon, policy-making levels of the state bureaucracy. An Albuquerque newspaper reported that of 1529 state employees earning $1,000 a month or more, 1,003 (66 percent) were Anglos and 516 (34 percent) were "Spanish Americans."[39]

Excuses for Lack of Representation

The majority of studies attempting to explain this lack of representation conclude that Chicanos could indeed gain and hold political office if only they learned to use the ballot effectively. Edward Banfield's discussion of Chicano political activities in El Paso is typical of this view: "The people who might be expected to want the most from an active city government—the poor Latins—are apathetic and politically ineffective."[40] Thus he and politicos justify ignoring the Chicano. "It's better to go to the shopping centers where the votes are than to mess around the pool halls of the South Side." Before attempting to determine whether or not Chicanos are indeed incapable of using the ballot box effectively, we would suggest examining exactly how the electoral process functions in relation to the Chicano.

The Electoral Process vs. Chicanos

A number of practices, purposely so designed or not, function to minimize or eliminate Chicano electoral success. The most flagrant of these include gerrymandering (arranging voting districts to give one group unfair advantage), voting requirements, at-large elections, and economic threats. As might be expected, the specific practice employed varies from region to region.

Gerrymandering

In California, gerrymandering has been the principal barrier preventing Chicanos from winning a proportionate number of offices. As of 1970 the Chicano community in East Los Angeles, where almost a million Chicanos reside, was sliced into nine state assembly districts, seven state senate districts, and six U.S. congressional districts. None of these is 40 percent Chicano.[41]

In 1971, Chicano community leaders attempted to have East Los Angeles redistricted to ensure safe Chicano seats. Initially, state Democratic leaders seemed receptive to the proposal, but after numerous delays they dropped redistricting plans and produced no new Mexican American districts. It is because of such practices that the U.S. Commission on Civil Rights concluded that "the Mexican American in California has been gerrymandered out of any real chance to elect his own representatives to the State Legislature or the United States Congress in a proportion approaching his percentage of the State population."[42]

At-Large Elections

In Texas and Arizona at-large elections have perhaps been the most effective tactic for diluting the impact of Chicano voters. The at-large election is used at a variety of levels including school districts, junior college districts, city council elections, and elections for state representatives. At-large elections provide Anglo voters numerous opportunities to defeat any Chicano candidate. Many candidates usually contest any given election, and seldom does an individual win a majority in the initial voting. Runoff elections thus provide Anglo voters the opportunity to mobilize behind whichever Anglo candidate is in the runoff. The result is that in these runoffs Chicano candidates usually lose even if they were the principal vote-getters in the primary elections. In Texas, because it is a one-party state, defeat in the Democratic runoff is tantamount to defeat in the general election.[43]

Multimember Districts

Multimember districts produce the same results because they function in essentially the same way. All the citizens in a given district vote for all the candidates, and thus one set of citizens can and often does elect all the representatives. Usually the representatives elected in these ways reside with and share the values of the Anglo middle class; Chicanos thus have no representation. It is for these reasons that the federal courts have recently found multimember districts to be a means of diluting the voting strength of Chicanos and ruled against them.[44]

Changing from multimember districts and at-large elections to single-member districts produced immediate beneficial results for the Texas Chicano community. Between 1960 and 1972, only twelve Chicanos were elected to the State House in eleven test counties, even though the Mexican American population in these areas ranged from 57 percent to 43 percent. In Bexar county, four Chicano representatives won office the first year single-member districts were put into effect; prior to 1972 only five Mexican Americans had ever won legislative seats in this county. "One does not have to employ sophisticated methodological techniques to reach the common sense conclusion that electoral arrangements have affected the outcome of elections . . . ."[45]

An additional problem confronting Chicanos considering running for office in such districts is the process by which candidates are selected to run. Because such districts have Anglo majorities, it is unlikely that parties will nominate minority candidates. This has clearly been the case in Texas. However, with the establishment of single-member districts, Chicanos are able to nominate minority candidates without any opposition. Consequently, in Texas the establishment of single-member districts saw an immediate increase in the number of Chicano candidates seeking office.[46]

Racial Bias

A less overt factor affecting elections across the Southwest is the subconscious and conscious racism with which voters view Chicano candidates. This racial bias is mobilized subtly through the use of code words such as "block voting."

Examples of bias. In El Paso, for example, a candidate who was attempting to be a spokesman for the Chicano community was described as a representative of "special interest," while his opponent who was representing an equally homogenous group of Anglos was described in the press as a "candidate of all the people."[47] The Republican and Democratic party chairmen admit that whisper campaigns are used to mobilize this bias.[48]

The impact of this bias is seen when Anglo voters join forces against Chicano candidates. In Travis county, Texas, a Chicano won the Democratic legislative primary with a 6,000 vote plurality over two Anglo opponents, who together received approximately 45,000 votes. In the runoff, the Chicano candidate gained less than 3,000 votes, while his opponent received over 9,000 new votes and won the election. The Chicano candidate lost the election even though he carried Chicano precincts with 90 percent plus margins.[49] State senate elections in El Paso, Texas produced similar results. The Chicano candidate led the primary, but in the runoff, Anglo voters supported the "candidate of all the people" almost totally, and the Chicano candidate went down to defeat.[50]

The depth of this racial bias is suggested by the attitudes with which many Anglos view Chicano candidates. In Lubbock, Texas, 24 percent of the Anglos disapproved of Mexican Americans serving as state representatives, 38 percent disapproved of a Mexican American governor, and 44 percent disapproved of the idea of a Mexican American president.[51] It is not difficult to imagine how such attitudes are translated into action in the privacy of a voting booth.

Need for Chicano majority. A corollary to the mobilization of racial bias is that unless electoral districts are designed to insure that they have majority Chicano populations, it is highly unlikely that Chicanos will be elected. A study of Texas political officials revealed, for example, that almost 80 percent of Chicano office holders were from South Texas, the area in which Chicanos are most highly concentrated, and 74 percent of these officials claimed a Mexican American constituency. Moreover, 64 percent of them were from small towns and rural areas, areas where the sheer force of numbers can not be denied.[52]

Chicano Solidarity vs. Mistrust

Chicanos elected from mixed districts or districts with a majority Anglo population must respond to mixed demands, or in the latter case to the demands of the Anglo voters. Such office holders are clearly not in a position to be strong advocates of Chicano causes. For this reason the electoral triumphs of Governor Castro, Governor Apodaca, Congressman Roybal, Congressman Lujan, and others, while significant, should not automatically be interpreted as major victories for the Chicano community.

Conflicting views. The fact that Mexican American office holders have often been responsive primarily either to Anglo political leaders or to white voters in general has taught Chicanos not to vote for a candidate merely because of a Spanish surname. This appropriate caution has had a devastating impact on efforts to establish a united Chicano front. On the one hand, Chicanos agree on the need to work together. In Los Angeles and San Antonio, 82 and 90 percent of the Chicano populations agreed that there should be ethnic unity.[53] On the other hand opportunistic individuals attempt to exploit this feeling to their own advantage, and probably to the advantage of non-Chicano political leaders who support these nonauthentic candidates and divide the Chicano vote.

In Denver, for example, while 51 percent of the Chicano population agreed that "any Mexican American city councilman would be better for this district than an Anglo," 31 percent disagreed.[54] That the majority of the population supported this proposition suggests the depth of alienation from core-culture politicians and of their support of ethnic solidarity. That almost a third oppose this suggestion indicates in part the distrust many Chicanos have of Mexican American officials because of former Chicano office holders who did not serve the community. This view also indicates that many Chicanos recognize that there are Anglo politicians who are trustworthy and supportive of their needs.

The meaning of Chicano voting behavior. Despite these divergent views, Chicanos usually attempt to counter white racial mobilization with a solid ethnic block vote. And without the overwhelming support of Chicano voters few Chicano candidates would ever win office. This does not mean that Chicanos vote exclusively for Spanish-surnamed candidates. When Chicanos have the opportunity to vote for a Chicano who will genuinely represent them, they do so. Between a Mexican American who is not supportive of Chicano issues and an Anglo who is, they will support the latter.[55]

Often, however, Chicanos must choose between an unattractive Anglo candidate and a Mexican American aspirant who has not openly committed himself to the resolution of community problems. In such cases, Chicanos simply stay away from the polls. This decision is often incorrectly interpreted as the community's unwillingness to support its own people. An accurate analysis of such behavior is that nonvoting in such cases documents the Chicano's political sophistication and unwillingness to support any candidate merely because he or she has a Spanish surname.[56]

The final most significant factor affecting Chicano voting patterns and electoral success is their relationship to the Democratic and Republican parties. The nature and extent of this problem will be discussed in the following chapter.

Conclusion

Of all the aspects of Chicano politics, the Chicano electoral experience is least susceptible to a simplistic analysis within any of our three models. Each model contributes something to our understanding of the process, but none explains it fully.

Internal colonialism explains well the obstacles used to prevent Chicanos from registering, voting, and winning office. Chicanos are kept poor and uneducated, insuring that they will show little interest in political affairs. Their social and economic conditions are such that even if they have the interest they will not have the time to devote to politics. If some Chicanos are able to overcome these barriers, they then encounter a series of mechanisms that minimize or eliminate any impact their electoral activities might have had. At-large elections, multimember districts, voting requirements, and other obstacles were designed to keep minorities from having political influence, and they have performed this function very well.

The internal colonial model, however, is unable to explain the recent changes that have occurred in Southwestern politics. It is the pluralistic model that best explains these. Now that Chicanos have learned to organize, they are beginning to win political office. It is through the effective use of the political process that Chicanos now hold 40 percent of the governorships in the Southwest and key state legislative positions in New Mexico, Arizona, and Colorado, and that they are becoming increasingly important in local politics throughout the area.

While it can not be denied that Chicanos faced serious obstacles in the past, these obstacles were similar to those faced by all ethnic groups in the United States. Now Chicanos, like the Irish and Polish before them, have learned to use the system, learned English and "Americanized" themselves, and are participating effectively within the system. As Chicanos become more educated and expand their political influence, greater and greater benefits will accrue to them. Soon Chicanos will be as much a part of the American electoral system as any other group.

Despite these recent changes, however, no real change has yet been seen in the living conditions of the masses of the Mexican American people. This lack of impact is best explained by the elite model. The elites are relatively unconcerned with the political activities of the Chicano population. They themselves are not threatened by Chicano politicians, and therefore it is not they who establish the obstacles to keep Chicanos out. The elites are concerned to protect their interests, and they do so through the exercise of economic power. So long as these Chicano politicians do not threaten the structure of the economic system, the elites will not intervene in their activities.

In other words, these electoral triumphs are insignificant to the elites. What is significant is that property relationships be maintained as they are. Since this is the case—since the poverty and employment problem has not been seriously attacked—the elites remain aloof from the political process. And there is no change in the living conditions of the Chicano community.

It seems, then, that Chiano electoral activities can not be seen within any one context. To analyze correctly the Chicano electoral experience it is necessary to use a variety of descriptive models and ultimately to formulate a new model that includes parts of each. Even then, Chicano electoral reality remains clouded. The electoral context has varied from one locale to another as it has also evolved through time. Electoral laws and regulations are still changing as the relationship between Chicanos and the majority society changes. Moreover, in the mid-1970s the electoral process itself has been subjected to increasing criticism and skepticism by Anglo Americans themselves. Because of this state of flux, no static model is adequate to encompass the Chicano electoral experience.

Chapter 7 Notes

1. Among the excellent works on elections and voting behavior in the United States are: Angus Campbell et al., *The American Voter* (New York: John Wiley, 1960); William H. Flanigan, *Political Behavior of the American Electorate*, 2nd ed. (Boston: Allyn and Bacon, 1972); and V. O. Key and Milton C. Cummings, *The Responsible Electorate* (Cambridge, Mass.: Harvard University Press, 1966. For an excellent, succinct review of the role of parties and elections in the United States, see Thomas R. Dye and L. Harmon Zeigler, *The Irony of Democracy* (North Scituate, Mass.: Duxbury Press, 1975), pp. 191-252.

2. Leonard Pitt, *Decline of the Californios* (Berkeley: University of California Press, 1966); Fernando V. Padilla and Carlos B. Ramirez, "Patterns of Chicano Representation in California, Colorado and Nuevo Mexico." *Aztlan* 5, nos. 1 & 2 (Spring and Fall 1974): 189-235.

3. Leo Grebler, Joan Moore, Ralph Guzman, *The Mexican American People* (New York: Free Press, 1970), p. 567.

4. Southwest Voter Registration Education Project: *Goals, Objectives, and Operations of the Southwest Voter Registration Education Project*, November 1974, p. 9.

5. Nicolas P. Lovrich, Jr., "Chicanos, Hispanos, Mexicans and Others: Political Attitudes and Ethnic Self-Identification Among Mexican American Voters," paper presented to the Rocky Mountain Social Science Association, April 1974, p. 6.

6. U.S. Census, *Current Population Reports*, no 253, 1972, p. 20.

7. Southwest Voter Registration, *Goals, Objectives, and Operations*, p. 10.

8. Lovrich, "Chicanos, Hispanos, Mexicans," p. 7.

9. U.S. Census, *Current Population Reports*, p. 20.

10. Maurilio E. Vigil, "An Analysis of the 1974 Gubernatorial Election in New Mexico" (unpublished paper, 1975).

11. Mark Levy and Michael Kramer, *The Ethnic Factor* (New York: Simon and Schuster, 1972), pp. 73-80.

12. Southwest Voter Registration, *Goals, Objectives, and Operations*, p. 6.

13. California State Advisory Commission on Civil Rights, *Political Participation of Mexican Americans in California*, August 1971, pp. 35-44.

14. John Staples Shockley, *Chicano Revolt in a Texas Town* (Notre Dame: University of Notre Dame Press, 1973) describes these retaliatory measures.

15. *Genoveva Cástro et al* vs. *State of California*, filed March 24, 1970, L.A. no. 29693.

16. California State Advisory Commission, *Political Participation of Mexican Americans*, p. 39.

17. Grebler, Moore, and Guzman, *The Mexican American People*, p. 567.

18. *Majority-Minority Citizen Voter Attitudes in Denver*, Denver Urban Observatory, Summer 1972, p. 20.

19. Ibid., p. 15.

20. Clifton McCleskey and Bruce Merrill, "Mexican American Political Behavior in Texas," *Social Science Quarterly*, 53, no. 4 (March 1973): 803-804.

21. Grebler et al., *The Mexican American People*, p. 567.

22. *Majority-Minority Citizen Voter Attitudes*, p. 36.

23. Ibid., p. 14.

24. Armando Rendon, *Chicano Manifesto* (New York: Macmillan, 1971), pp. 26-27.

25. Ralph C. Guzman, *The Political Socialization of the Mexican American People* (Ph.D. dissertation, University of California, Los Angeles, 1969).

26. Southwest Voter Registration, *Goals, Objectives, and Operations*, p. 7.

27. Ibid., p. 7.

28. *LULAC News*, 1974 (undated publication), p. 8.

29. Professor Maurilio Vigil of New Mexico Highlands University has statistically demonstrated that the deciding factor in Governor Apodaca's slight

edge for victory was his very strong voting support from the Hispanic counties in northern New Mexico. See his "An Analysis of the 1974 Gubernatorial Elections in New Mexico."

30. Padilla and Ramirez, "Patterns of Chicano Representation," pp. 191-202.

31. Ibid., pp. 203-210.

32. Ibid., p. 210.

33. John Crow, "Mexican American Wards and Tucson City Elections," (undated paper, University of Arizona), pp. 3-4.

34. Shockley, *Chicano Revolt*, describes the resistance to continued Chicano electoral triumph in southern Texas.

35. California State Advisory Commission, *Political Participation of Mexican Americans.*

36. Adaljiza Sosa Riddell, "Local Elites, Local Policy and Political Change: The Case of Parlier, California" (paper presented at the 1975 Western Political Science Association convention).

37. Norton Long, as quoted in Rudolph Gomez, "Mexican Americans in American Bureaucracy," in *Mexican Americans: Political Power, Influence or Resource*, ed. Frank Baird (Lubbock: Texas Tech Press, 1976.)

38. California State Advisory Commission, *Political Participation of Mexican Americans*, pp. 80-88.

39. *Albuquerque Journal*, May 23, 1975, p. 1.

40. Edward Banfield, *Big City Politics* (New York: Random House, 1965, pp. 70-71.

41. California State Advisory Commission, *Political Participation of Mexican Americans.*

42. Ibid., p. 8.

43. The impact of at-large elections on Chicano voting is discussed at length in Charles L. Cotrell, "The Effects of At-Large Elections on the Political Access and Voting Strength of Mexican Americans and Blacks in Texas" (paper presented at the Rocky Mountain Social Science Association Meeting), April 1974.

44. Ibid., p. 2.

45. Ibid., p. 26.

46. Ibid., p. 29-30.

47. Rudolph O. de la Garza, "Voting Patterns in 'Bi-Cultural' El Paso: A Contextual Analysis of Mexican American Voting Behavior," *Aztlan* 5, nos. 1 and 2 (Spring and Fall 1974): 235-260.

48. Cotrell, "The Effects of At-Large Elections," p. 50.

49. Ibid., p. 43.

50. De la Garza, "Voting Patterns in 'Bi-Cultural' El Paso," p. 254.

51. As cited in Cotrell, "The Effects of At-Large Elections," p. 46.

52. José Angel Gutiérrez, *El Político* (El Paso: Mictla, 1972), p. 17.

53. Grebler, Moore, and Guzman, *The Mexican American People*, p. 568.

54. *Majority-Minority Citizen Voter Attitudes*, p. 94.

55. Rudolph O. de la Garza, "Mexican American Voters: A Responsible Electorate," in *Mexican Americans: Political Power, Influence or Resource*, ed. Frank Baird (Lubbock: Texas Tech Press).

56. Ibid.

Chicanos and the Politics of Coalitions and Political Parties:

"Comida hecha, compania desecha."*

A time-tested way to exert influence in a political system is to form coalitions with other individuals or groups so as to combine resources and thus increase the political power of all coalition members. A related strategy involves committing a group's resources to a political party with the expectation that this will result in that party distributing rewards to its supporters once that party has attained power. These tactics are advantageous to any group, but they are particularly beneficial to the least powerful.

Coalitions

Chicanos would gain greatly from entering into coalitions with other groups. Chicanos are a minority nationwide, in every state, and in many communities. Coalitions with other groups would at least increase their voting strength, adding all-essential numbers to their minority. In several southwestern cities, for example, a coalition of Indians and Chicanos could constitute a majority and be quite successful in winning elections.

Need for Coalition

As we have already pointed out, the Chicano people do not have financial resources comparable to those of core culture groups. But this comparatively low level of wealth could be raised by increasing the number of people who could add their meager resources to a combined political war chest. Ten thousand people giving five dollars are financially equal to five wealthy contributors donating $10,000.

Another political resource, time to devote to political pursuits, is scarce among the Chicano people, since most of them are busily engaged in simple survival and earning a living. But more people giving small amounts of time could add up to a substantial block of time,

*"The meal over, the guests depart."

even though it is probably more efficient to have one full-time political activist than five part-time people.

We also saw Chicanos had relatively little representation among elected officials, an important resource. A coalition of a few Chicanos with other elected officials could certainly increase block strength at the decision-making level. Thus in general the idea of Chicanos joining forces with other groups would seem to be a good idea.

Conditions for Coalition

There are certain conditions which must be fulfilled before any kind of a coalition can be successful.[1] The first is that the partners of a coalition must agree on the basic goal of the alliance. This is often a difficult first step. It would be easiest to coalesce around a broad, rather vaguely defined goal. However, such a goal leads to problems of strategy, since the direction of the political movement would only vaguely defined. It also make it difficult to know when the goal has been achieved. On the other hand, a specific objective, while effectively channeling the efforts of the coalition, makes forming a coalition much more difficult. But broadly or narrowly defined, the goal must be one that all interested parties see as very desirable. This is so because in general the groups must perceive the costs of joining in a coalition as outweighed by the benefits.

One of the major costs involved would be that of compromise—an element essential to the combining of any set of forces. A group may have to expand or limit its objectives and would most probably have to sacrifice some material benefit, ideological purity, or cultural homogeneity. It is also important to the success of any coalition that the parties to the alliance be relatively equal in strength. If the member groups are substantially unequal in resources, problems usually arise. The dominant group begins to dictate the terms of the alliance and ignores the wishes of the less influential groups. The less powerful groups become quite unhappy and frustrated because their wishes are put in secondary positions. Only among relatively equal groups can compromise and bargaining take place.

Potential Allies

Given these general observations, who might be the most suitable potential allies for the Chicano? The answer that most readily comes to mind is other nonwhite ethnics such as the Native Americans or Afro-Americans.

Native Americans. There is much to be said for a coalition between Chicanos and Native Americans, for these groups seem to have much in common.[2] The *mestizo* symbol of the Chicano* includes the combination of his Spanish father and Indian mother, so there are blood ties between the two groups. The groups coexist in the American West. Both Chicanos and Indians are at the very bottom of the socioeconomic ladder of the United States, sharing similar conditions of poverty, poor education, poor housing, poor health, and unemployment.

There are some quite similar cultural features of each group. Perhaps most important is their relationship to the land. Both groups until recently have been rural, and their values are reflected in their attitudes towards the land as something to be worked, to be held in trust for the use of others, rather than a commodity to be bought and sold. Both groups are currently migrating into the urban areas in great numbers.

Perhaps most important is their historical experience, for both groups fit very well the colonial analogy. Both were pre-Anglo inhabitants of this southwestern area, were conquered by military forces of the United States, and were regulated by treaties establishing the relationships between the United States and both Chicanos and Indians. The culture of each has been treated with disrespect, and both groups have suffered a great deal of racial discrimination.

There are, of course, some problems in formulating a brown-red political coalition. Historically, there has been conflict between the two groups, particularly in the early period of Spanish and Mexican exploration of the southwestern United States. Perhaps most importantly, the fact that both groups have been placed at the bottom by Anglo-American society has resulted in an unfortunate but common psychological consequence. That is, one subordinated group attempts to look down on the other group in order to feel that it has bettered itself relatively. Much as the Southern white "redneck" considers himself automatically superior to the black, Chicanos have sometimes looked down upon Indians, attempting to raise themselves through the use of the dominant society's standards. The competition for material resources also tends to pit Chicano against Indian. Since the majority society sets aside for minorities only a small proportion of

---

*A "combination face" made up of three – a Chicano full face forward, a left-side view of the Indian mother, and a right-side view of the Spanish father.

the available resources, the two minority groups quarrel over these small rewards.

Nevertheless there have been several examples of Chicano-Indian alliances. For example, in 1968 the Alianza (the group formed by Tijerina to get back the Mexican and Spanish land grants) ran a slate of officers for election in New Mexico under the People's Constitutional Party. Its candidate for governor was the head of the Alianza, Reies Lopez Tijerina. When the courts declared Tijerina ineligible as a political candidate because he was then under indictment for some of his Alianza activities, the party nominated in his place an Indian, José Maestas. This of course tied in well with the Alianza's emphasis on the new *mestizo* race of Indo-Hispanos. Some of the campuses in the Southwest have featured Chicano-Indian coalitions in elections for student government positions. At least at this level coalitions can be quite successful, as several student governments of colleges in the Southwest have been taken over by minority groups.

Blacks. Another possibility for Chicanos would be a coalition with blacks. American blacks are also at the lowest level of the socioeconomic ladder and have suffered severe discrimination on account of their race at the hands of the core culture. They too were recently rural and have within the last generation or two become predominantly an urban people centered in the run-down areas of cities. Thus a Chicano-Afro coalition might seem to have a ready base for alliance. However, there may be some problems in bringing about a Chicano-black alliance.

The histories of the two groups are quite different, the most common features being their general treatment by the Anglo society. Afro-Americans were not original inhabitants of the area which became the United States. They did not have in this country thriving communities with a whole range of political, religious, and economic institutions, as did the Indian and Chicano. Their culture was largely destroyed as they were brought in slavery to the United States. Chicanos and Indians, for example, have retained their native languages while blacks generally speak only English. In short, the cultural values of blacks may be more similar to those of the core-culture Americans than those of Chicanos. Another problem is that, as in the case of the Native American, the Afro-American has been pitted against the Chicano in a contest over the droppings from the higher levels of the American society.

The Mexican American Study Project out of the University of California at Los Angeles found that the idea of a political coalition with blacks was rejected by three-fourths of the Chicano respondents in their San Antonio and Los Angeles survey.[3] Chicanos disagreed that "Mexican Americans should get together with Negros politically." Reasons for that attitude might include Chicanos' feeling that their situation and their group is unique, having a very different historical experience from that of blacks, the perceived differences in the problems of the two groups, some prejudice against blacks fostered by the core society, the fear of the dilution of the *unidad* (unity) concept among Chicanos, and the usual psychological results of the colonizers' divide-and-conquer tactics.

Indicative of the differences between Chicanos and blacks is the way in which each views the issue of busing and school desegregation in general. As the Boston school crisis still going on at this writing illustrates, the black community is strongly in favor of integrating schools through busing or other means. Chicanos, however, are less concerned with busing and desegregation than with quality education, and they believe they can attain their goal without integrating themselves into the core culture. Furthermore, it is very likely that many Chicanos resist busing and forced integration because this would destroy Chicano neighborhoods and community. For whatever the reason, Table 8-1, documents the significant differences between the two groups on this issue.

Many Chicanos also seem to reject the black militant strategy as incompatible with the Chicano sense of dignity. Corky Gonzáles, a leading Chicano militant, described this reaction:

> Why do blacks riot? Because they see no way out, because they feel trapped in the ghettoes, because that is how mass society acts. I respect the suffering of the blacks. We both have suffered. We work together. But we work differently because we are a different people. Our culture is such that we don't like to march, to protest. We don't like to be conspicuous. We don't like to seem ridiculous in the public eye. That is machismo. We are not nonviolent. But in the barrio self-determination means that every man, every people, every barrio has to be able to take care of themselves, with dignity. We are men of silent violence.[4]

Although Corky Gonzáles, has since changed his views and behavior, his statement continues to echo the feelings of most Mexican Americans. In Denver in 1972, for example, only 27 percent of the Chicano community agreed that violence is sometimes necessary to overcome barrio conditions; 52 percent of the blacks agreed with this.[5]

Table 8-1
Chicano and Black Attitudes Toward Busing and School Integration, Denver, 1972

Busing	*Black*	*Mexican American*
Favor	67 percent	25 percent
Oppose	23 percent	66 percent
Improve neighborhood schools instead of directing efforts to achieve ethnic balance		
Favor	69 percent	84 percent
Oppose	18 percent	6 percent

Source: Majority-Minority Citizen Voter Attitudes in Denver, Denver Urban Observatory, 1972, p. 51.

In spite of these obstacles there have been some examples of Chicano-Afro political coalitions. For example, in the middle and late sixties Chicanos organized in PASO (Political Association of Spanish Speaking Organizations) affiliated with black organizations in San Antonio and Houston in order to elect minority group members to office. In the farm workers' struggle several black civil rights organizations have contributed their resources to *La Causa*. La Raza Unida Party in Texas has several times endorsed and worked for black political candidates.

There have been some examples of failures in attempts to join forces, too. In the 1968 mayoral race in Los Angeles Chicanos supported the long-time mayor, Sam Yorty, instead of the black mayoral candidate, Tom Bradley. The Chicano vote could have made Bradley mayor. Increasing political sophistication, perhaps including a heightened realization of their common situation, led Chicano voters in 1972 to support Bradley in his renewed attempt to oust Yorty. This time the Chicano vote, along with diminished white support for Yorty, elected Thomas Bradley to the chief executive position in the nation's second largest city.[6]

Working-class whites. Another potential major coalition would be that between Chicanos and working-class whites. Indeed, according to a Marxist analysis of history, a class alliance would be the most effective in changing the system. However, this "natural" alliance has not yet formed and there is little evidence that it is currently forming. The issues of race and culture seem to loom too large. Just as in the South poor white and black political alliances were not formed, and in fact the poor white was often the greatest opponent of black equality, in the West the situation seems to be very similar for the Chicano.

There has been a long history of conflict between Chicanos and whites in the West, and this historical antagonism is difficult to put aside even on the grounds of basic economic similarities. There is some evidence that the lower-class whites may be the most anti-Chicano, since lower-class whites and Chicanos are placed in competition for the low-grade jobs that are available to them as well as for educational scholarships and other welfare services. Much of the opposition to the government's so-called "quotas" or "goals" for increased opportunities to racial minorities has come from envious working-class whites. They feel neglected and discriminated against since they are overlooked and by-passed in some of the federal "minority opportunity" programs.

Upper- and middle-class whites. Paradoxical though it may seem, examples of "successful" coalitions between whites and Chicanos usually involve upper-middle-class and upper-class whites, mainly those with liberal or radical beliefs. The problem of racial prejudice still exists, of course, and the resource inequality in this kind of combination can cause the problems discussed above. Additionally, white liberals and radicals have unknowingly displayed a paternalistic attitude towards ethnic allies. Sometimes their organizational experience and skills have pushed them towards leadership roles in political alliances.

The key question is: are the interests of the white liberal or radical and the Chicano really the same? There is of course a great difference in their material status. Upper-class white liberals and radicals are past worrying about clothes, shelter, education, health services—things for which the Chicano is very much striving. The antimaterialist proclamation of many white liberals and radicals seems a facade to many Chicanos because these same liberals or radicals support Chicano demands only when it is convenient for them. When hard choices have to be made and sides chosen, the white liberal or radical often sides with the dominant society. Thus in 1972 the liberal Democratic candidate for governor in Texas, Sissy Farenthold, endorsed conservative Democrat Dolph Briscoe, who defeated her in the party primary, rather than support the Raza Unida candidate, who ran on a platform almost identical with Farenthold's (see p. 174).

An example of this difference is the great decline in Jewish support for black attempts to advance themselves in late sixties and early seventies. Prosperous Jews had always played an important role in the black civil rights movement, providing organizational skills and financial resources to black groups. However, when the civil rights phase of the movement had attained its goals with the passage of legislation in 1964 and 1965, the black struggle for substantive rather than legal equality and liberation began. Blacks began using nonconventional tactics, including violence, and espousing cultural values, and they lost much of their Jewish support. The idea of minority quotas in employment, education, etc. seems to be an anathema to many Jewish liberals, and of course Jews are perceived by colored minorities as part of the white dominant society.

Nevertheless, one can recall the work that Saul Alinsky and Fred Ross, for example, did in the early days of the Community Service Organization (CSO) in California. In the farm workers' movement, much support was gathered from the upper ranks of labor; Walter Ruether of the United Auto Workers was one of the staunchest supporters of César Chávez and his movement. Robert Kennedy became very interested in the plight of the farm workers and made a great contribution both financially and through his moral support. Mayor Joseph Alioto of San Francisco and Mayor John Lindsay of New York both took public stands in support of the UFWOC. The California Migrant Ministry and later the United States Conference of Catholic Bishops both played important supportive roles in the farm worker's movement. In addition, radical-liberal students, from California's universities such as Berkeley in particular, worked side by side with the farm workers in their organizational and picketing and boycott activities.

In the New Mexico Alianza, William Higgs, a lawyer who had been active in the civil rights movement in the South, provided invaluable legal assistance to Tijerina's Alianza activities. In the 1963 elections in Crystal City, Texas, support of working class Chicanos by the Teamster's Union and white liberals made possible the election of Chicanos to all five city council seats in Crystal City. So under some conditions and specific circumstances a brown-white political coalition can be effective.[7]

Chicanos and Party Politics

All of the problems, advantages, and disadvantages of coalition building become apparent and even exaggerated in the functioning of the American two-party system. The American political process and the two-party system enjoy a symbiotic relationship—each reinforces and nurtures the other. Thus the American parties offer the most direct channel to political influence, office and power. This is not to say that the parties are easily accessible. They are, however, more accessible than other national political institutions, and therefore all groups with political objectives must deal with them in one way or another.

Advantages in Working with the System

Working within the American two-party system offers several key advantages to any group.

General advantages. Most significantly, the American public grants legitimacy to the activities, platforms, and candidates of both parties. Efforts to engage in political affairs outside of these structures, either through direct action or through a third party, are viewed with suspicion and consequently are seldom successful. As popularly based organizations, the dominant parties are able to mobilize their members in support of party positions, and thus they are in a good position to influence policy makers and win elections. As broad-based coalitions of like-minded people, they provide a much-needed stability to the political process.

In terms of policy formulation, this means that parties modify the specific demands of member groups so as to increase the probability of these demands being accepted by the membership and the public in general. Finally, America's dominant parties offer opportunities to express demands at a national level, to have demands incorporated into policy decisions, and to have representatives of the various groups within the party seek and win key political office. In other words, it is through the parties that groups can have their candidates become decision makers.

Advantages to Chicanos. In addition to these advantages, Chicanos could in principle gain specific benefits if they cooperated with the dominant parties. Because they are a minority population without a national audience, working with a political party would allow Chicanos to reach audiences they have not reached to date. It is likely that popular support would be mobilized in support of Chicano demands if either the Republican or Democratic party were to express these through official channels. Furthermore, the funds, expertise, full-time staff and access to valuable information available within the party structures could be put to use to help the Chicano cause. If the party mobilized in behalf of Chicanos, much of the overt discrimination and abuse directed against the Chicano would probably be eliminated. Most public officials are members of one of the dominant parties, and it is unlikely that they would continue to discriminate against Chicanos if their party or their major opposition openly and strongly criticized such actions.

Having dominant party support would also help to mobilize the alienated sections of the Chicano community. Such support would demonstrate that the system was in fact becoming responsive to the Chicano, and under such conditions it is much more likely that Chicanos would develop a sense that their political actions had some effect. Dominant party support would also help to eliminate or minimize any fears Chicanos might have of becoming openly involved in politics.Without such support, Chicanos are left at the mercy of the institutions which have abused them for generations.

Access to decision makers. Perhaps the most immediately significant advantage of working with either of the dominant parties is that through them Chicanos would have access to the highest level decision makers in all political and governmental institutions. The great majority of our governmental bodies are organized or function along party lines. Party organizations and leaders, for example, play a major part in the organization and functioning of state and national legislatures. Party officials such as majority and minority whips, the leaders of the respective party caucuses, and the majority and minority leaders exert substantial influence in legislative affairs. Committee assignments and activities also reflect partisan division. The impact of party considerations is even more immediate in executive positions such as governorships, mayoralties, and the presidency. Without the assistance of the major political parties, Chicanos are unlikely to have any influence in these offices.

Disadvantages in Working with the System

But there are disadvantages as well as advantages to working with a major political party. Because our political parties are broad-based coalitions of interests, any single group must usually compromise its position tremendously in order to become part of this mass coalition. A culturally homogeneous and distinct group will have to sacrifice much of its valued differences in order to be satisfied with and play an effective role in the policies of a major party. The two major parties would have a hard time incorporating any distinctive Chicano demands, since the parties are based on the Anglo tradition of ethnic groups' subordination to the melting-pot—that is, conforming to Anglo culture. This would, of course, be less true at the county and local level than at the national or state level.

Moreover, Chicanos, as a minority element, risk being swallowed up by other interests or subordinated to the interests of other parts of these grand coalitions. Chicanos are a minority nationally and statewide as well as within the Republican and Democratic Parties. They might thus be ignored by a major party; if they are a small minority, they might not be needed. Membership in a major party also decreases the flexibility and adaptability or the "room for maneuver" by an independent force such as the Chicano. Once within an organization some degree of following the principles, rules, and practices of the group is necessary. Thus, several options for the Chicano would be no longer available.

Chicano Dealings with Democrats

How Chicanos have dealt with the two-party system is unclear. As with every other aspect of Chicano politics, numerous misconceptions and myths about the relationship of Chicanos to the dominant parties have become accepted as dogma. Existing studies assert that Chicanos simply do not understand how to deal with the party system, that they are unquestionably supportive of the Democrats, that they do not know how to court both parties to see which is willing to offer the most in return for Chicano support, and that both parties are equally unresponsive to the Chicano.[8] These assertions are simply not supported by available data. In fact, an analysis of the relationship between Chicanos and America's dominant parties systematically disproves each of these claims.

Loyalty to Democrats. It is true that Chicanos work closely and identify with the Democratic party. In Texas, 86 percent of Chicano voters identify with the Democratic party;[9] 86 percent of Chicanos in Denver also identify as Democrats.[10] This is not to say, however, that Chicanos are blindly loyal to one party. Only 41 percent of the Texas Chicanos, for example, consider themselves "strong Democrats," and only 35 percent vote a straight Democratic ticket.[11]

Given the history of American politics in general and southwestern politics in particular, it is not surprising that Chicanos are overwhelmingly Democratic. Under the leadership of Franklin Delano

Roosevelt, it was the Democratic party that initiated programs designed to aid the poor, and since almost all Chicanos were among the poor, they benefited greatly from these programs. Since then, Chicanos have "inherited" a loyalty to the Democratic party. Congressman Roybal's experiences illustrate this process:

> I think that the Roosevelt era really made me a Democrat. I remember the suffering under the Hoover administration and then I remember that we were losing our home . . . . I remember that during the Roosevelt administration they passed a homeowner's loan corporation that made it possible for us to keep our home. My father was, at that time, able to get work—WPA or whatever it was.[12]

This Chicano experience is similar to that of the blacks who became strongly pro-Republican after the Civil War and continued as Republicans until the Roosevelt era. The Irish, finding themselves courted by the minority Democratic party challenging the established Republicans, have also retained their Democratic allegiances for decades.

Moreover, in the Southwest the Democrats have long dominated political life. In effect, then, Chicanos usually had nowhere else to turn. In states where one party dominates, it is nonsensical to attempt to negotiate with the nondominant party.

Alternatives. It is noteworthy that when alternatives did exist, Chicanos chose them. This is most evident in New Mexico.[13] Early in the history of the state, Chicanos were more closely affiliated with the Republicans than with the Democrats. Since the 1930s, however, there has been a rapid, continuous shift in party loyalty. By the 1960s, Chicanos had almost completely abandoned the Republican party in favor of the Democrats. Nonetheless, even today New Mexico's only Spanish-surnamed congressman is a Republican. Table 8-2 illustrates the shift in party loyalty since 1930.

Table 8-2
Party Affiliation of Chicano State Legislators
in New Mexico, 1930-1969.

	Republican	*Democrat*	*Total*
1930-1939	50	49	99
1940-1949	25	58	93
1950-1959	15	54	69
1960-1969	8	78	86

Source: Adapted from: Fernando V. Padilla and Carlos B. Ramirez, "Patterns of Chicano Representation in California, Colorado and Nuevo Mexico," *Aztlan,* Vol. 5, nos. 1 & 2 (Spring & Fall, 1974) p. 225.

Colorado. Chicanos in Colorado have made comparable use of both parties. Between 1914 and 1948, eighty-three Chicanos sought legislative office. Of the fifteen who won, nine were Democrats and six were Republicans. Of those who lost, thirty were Republicans and twenty-five were Democrats. Between 1959 and 1972, an additional fifty-eight Chicanos sought legislative office. Of thirty-seven Democratic candidates, twelve triumphed; only one of fourteen Chicano Republicans won.[14]

California. In this state, Chicanos have been much less successful in using the two-party system.[15] Of twenty-nine Chicanos who have been elected to legislative office, all but four have been Democrats. Between 1964 and 1973, eleven Chicanos ran for the state senate. The ten Chicano Democrats lost in the party primaries; the lone Republican lost in the general elections. In 1963 two Chicanos were elected to the lower house. Five more have been elected to the state assembly since that time. Recently, there has been greater parity in the number of Chicano candidates nominated for congressional office. Between 1962 and 1970, each party nominated seven Chicanos. Within the party, moreover, it seems that Chicanos face fewer obstacles as Republicans than as Democrats. Chicano Democratic nominees have always faced Anglo opponents in the party primaries; four of seven Chicano Republicans ran unopposed in the primary.

Arizona. Comparable patterns exist in Arizona. Democrats nominate Chicanos only when it is impossible to avoid doing so. Thus, as stated earlier, southern Arizona regularly sends Chicano representatives to the state legislature. Governor Raul Castro, however, did not receive party support in his quest for the governorship in 1972. Despite the party's disinterest in and even opposition to his candidacy, Castro almost won that election and established himself as an almost certain winner for the 1974 election. Unable to deny his candidacy, the Democratic hierarchy mobilized behind him in 1974 and assured his election.

Texas. In this state, the Democratic party has been extremely resistant to Chicano penetration. The fact that the Democrats completely dominate politics in that state means that Chicanos cannot turn anywhere else for support. Confident in their domination, Democrats have been content to ignore Chicano demands at local, state, and congressional levels.

Chicano Dealings with Republicans

While historically Republicans have been relatively uninterested in the Chicano vote, this situation changed temporarily during former

President Nixon's tenure in office.

The Nixon administration. In the early seventies the Nixon administration did make some attempts to win over the Chicano vote to the Republican side.[16] This was particularly true following Nixon's 1968 election when he was looking forward to the 1972 contest. Several Chicanos were appointed to relatively high-ranking positions in the Nixon administrations, even though very important top-level positions, at the secretarial level, for example, were not offered to Chicanos. Additionally, the hearings associated with the Watergate affair revealed that the Nixon administration set out purposefully to provide federal grants for programs that would specifically help the Chicano community.

The "southwestern strategy" enjoyed some success. Former President Nixon received more Mexican American votes than had any previous Republican candidate. Furthermore, fellow Republican John Tower also garnered many Chicano votes and actually carried counties with large Chicano populations.[17]

Loss of Chicano support. This support and the relatively numerous Chicano appointments made by the Nixon administration have produced few material benefits for the Chicano community, and it seems that the Chicano-Republican alliance is now a thing of the past; that is, Republicans are no longer actively seeking Chicano support. Recently Congressman Manuel Lujan of New Mexico was appointed head of a Republican committee whose purpose was to improve relationships with the Spanish-speaking community. The great loss of support following the Watergate affair and related controversies seem to be scaring the Republicans into turning their attention once more to the Chicano community. The present growing dissatisfaction of Chicanos with their position in the political system may be a tremendous untapped resource for the GOP. In New Mexico particularly, their victories might encourage them to exert the effort necessary to win over the Chicano voter. They might take favorable policy positions and more importantly implement these positions with effective programs.

Republican hostility. However, the stances taken by GOP administrations have usually been in conflict with the economic and cultural desires of most Chicanos. For example, former Republican Governor Jack Williams of Arizona alienated the entire Chicano community with his disregard of the demands made by United Farm Worker organizers. He signed into law a viciously anti-farm worker bill, and when asked to reconsider his actions, he replied, "As far as I am concerned, these people don't exist." Former Governor Reagan of California behaved similarly toward the farm workers, and received wide publicity as eating grapes during the boycott. So long as men such as Reagan hold positions of leadership within the GOP, it is unlikely that the Republicans will mount a serious effort to win Chicano support. And without such an effort, it is unlikely that Chicanos could ever support the Republican party.

Nonsupport of Democrats. That Chicanos do not blindly support the Democrats is further documented by the recent actions of Chicano political groups across the Southwest. In California, the Mexican American Political Association and the Congress of Mexican American Unity refused to endorse the Democratic nominee for governor in 1970.[18] In San Antonio, Chicano militants were instrumental in the defeat of Democratic state senator José Bernal. In 1971 in northern California Chicano opposition to a Democratic state assemblyman was instrumental in electing a Republican from a predominantly Democratic district.[19]

The Lesser of Two Evils

Thus, there is no truth to the suggestion that Chicanos do not know how to form alliances or work with the two-party system. In view of the existing political realities, the Chicanos have worked extremely well with both parties. It is the parties and not the Chicanos who have refused to cooperate. The Chicanos have supported whichever party was willing to deal with them, and they have demonstrated a willingness to switch their support from one party to another under the proper conditions. That they have been unable to penetrate the party structures more effectively cannot therefore be blamed on them.

One final proposition that must be refuted is that there is no difference between the way in which Republicans and Democrats respond to the Chicano. It is true that neither party has been primarily or actively concerned with Chicano problems. This, however, is not the same as saying that both parties relate to Chicanos in identical ways. Although the Democrats have not responded to Chicano demands, the Republicans have a record of openly attacking the Chicano community. Richard Nixon, like Reagan, made a public display of eating grapes at a time when the Chicano community was organizing a grape boycott. Former Governor Jack Williams' actions have already been described.

No Democrat has taken comparable actions, and many have acted in exactly opposite ways. Governor Richard Lamm of Colorado, for example, in 1975 actively supported a bilingual-bicultural education bill which would greatly aid Chicano children. Governor Gerald Brown of California has pushed through the state legislature a bill supporting César Chávez's farm workers. The support Robert Kennedy gave to Chicanos also illustrates this point. Furthermore, the Southwest's two Spanish-surnamed governors are Democrats and in New Mexico all but one of the Chicano state legislators are Democrats.

Again, what must be emphasized here is not that the Democrats have been open and receptive to Chicanos. They have not. They have often resisted demands for change and stood idly by while Chicanos made every effort to improve their life situation. The Republicans, however, in addition to resisting demands for change and standing by while Chicanos struggle to improve themselves, have actually taken actions to undermine Chicano efforts. Yet, no Republican leader has ever attempted to represent the Chicano community as did Robert Kennedy.

Conclusion

Elitist Analysis

The elite model of American politics does not explicitly address itself to details such as those described in this chapter. The model posits that elections are meaningless, and therefore the means for winning elections, such as forming alliances and working through political parties, are of no concern unless the objectives of such activities are the fundamental restructuring of the political and economic system. The alliances described here are clearly nonradical in nature and therefore unthreatening to the dominant elites. The dominant political parties by definition reinforce existing structures, and therefore any group's efforts to enlist their support are also nonthreatening.

Pluralist Analysis

The pluralist approach, on the other hand, can accommodate most of the developments described here. The fact that Chicanos enter into coalitions with some groups and not with others is predictable. The competition between blacks and Chicanos is typical of earlier competitions between other ethnic groups. As was true of those groups,

Chicanos must be willing to sacrifice some of their objectives and compromise on others in order to make meaningful alliances. When they have been willing to do so, such alliances have produced good results. It is because Chicanos are unwilling to make such concessions that they have not been more successful.

The fact that Chicanos have worked with both parties also supports the validity of the pluralist model. As the Republican party showed itself unwilling to respond to Chicano demands, the Democratic party stepped in and won the allegiance of the Mexican American community. By the 1970s, Republican leaders recognized that they could benefit from regaining Chicano support, and so they launched a campaign to this end. The campaign was short-lived, however, because Chicanos realized that the Republican party was not genuinely concerned with their problems. Meanwhile, aware that they could no longer take Chicanos for granted, the Democrats began recruiting, nominating, and electing Chicano candidates. The results of this effort can be seen in the election of Chicano Democratic governors in New Mexico and Arizona and of substantially more Chicano state legislators across the Southwest. Through these officials Chicanos will make rapid and important progress toward their goals.

Internal Colonialism Analysis

Internal colonialism does not offer genuinely satisfactory interpretations of these events. The model asserts that existing political structures keep Chicanos out of office, yet not only do Chicanos hold office, but both parties have sought at various times to incorporate Chicanos into the political process. Leaders of the Democratic party have openly defended Chicano demands, and Anglo Democratic officials are using the prestige and power of office to pass legislation supporting Chicano needs.

This model also asserts that there is no difference between the parties in terms of their dealing with the Mexican American community. As we have shown, such an assertion is simply incorrect. While neither party is challenging the foundations of the system, the Democratic party is clearly the more receptive to Chicanos.

Internal colonialism does, however, lend valuable insight into some problems Chicanos confront in attempting to build coalitions. The disputes between Chicanos and blacks, and Chicanos and Native Americans, while partially reflective of cultural differences, are to a greater degree the result of competition between the groups for scarce resources. The model clearly indicates how these groups can be mobilized against each other, and many examples following the model exist. Anglo elites, in other words, skillfully employ divide-and-conquer techniques that keep Chicanos isolated from other equally deprived groups.

Like the elite model, internal colonialism denies the significance of changes in the relationship between the dominant parties and Chicanos. And it is true that at the national level neither party has committed itself to supporting the Chicano community. Until such support is forthcoming—and there is no evidence that it is—the basic problems of the Chicano will go unresolved.

All three models, then, contribute to our understanding of the problems Chicanos face in developing coalitions and working with political parties. While each adds insights to the problems, the pluralistic analysis seems the most useful. Nonetheless, the questions raised by the internal colonial analysis must be answered.

Chapter 8
Notes

1. Conditions that work both for and against successful ethnic group coalitions have been forcefully presented by Stokely Carmichael and Charles V. Hamilton, *Black Power:The Politics of Liberation in America* (New York: Random House, 1967), pp. 58-84.

2. The similarities between Mexican and Native Americans are summed up in the term "territorial minorities" developed by Rudolph O. de la Garza, Z. Anthony Kruszewski, and Thomas A. Arciniega, *Chicanos and Native Americans: The Territorial Minorities* (New York: Prentice-Hall, 1973).

3. Leo Grebler, Joan W. Moore, and Ralph Guzman, *The Mexican-American People: The Nation's Second Largest Minority* (New York: The Free Press, 1970), pp. 568-69. In their 1972 follow-up study of the 1965 UCLA Project, Biliana Ambrecht and Harry Panchon found that the proportion of Mexican Americans favoring a strategy of coalition with blacks had more than doubled, from 16 percent to 39 percent. However, a majority of these respondents still opposed the idea; see their "Ethnic Political Mobilization in A Mexican American Community: An Exploratory Study of East Los Angeles, 1965-1972," *The Western Political Quarterly* 28, no. 3 (September 1974): 513-514. Jose M. Vadi, in his survey of a California barrio, also found less than majority support for a brown-black coalition; see his "Political Attitudes of Mexican Americans: Political Power, Influence or Resource," Texas Tech University, Lubbock, Texas, April 1974).

4. In Stan Steiner, *La Raza: The Mexican Americans* (New York: Harper & Row, 1970), p. 391.

5. *Majority-Minority Citizen Voter Attitudes in Denver*, Denver Urban Observatory, 1972, p. 51.

6. Empirical evidence supporting these speculations about changing attitudes has been provided by a follow-up study of the original respondents in the Mexican American Project. While in 1965 only 16 percent thought Mexican Americans should get together politically with blacks, by 1972 the proportion had more than doubled to 39 percent. Biliana C. S. Ambrecht and Harry P. Pachon, "Ethnic Political Mobilization in a Mexican American Community: An Exploratory Study of East Los Angeles, 1965-1972," *Western Political Quarterly* 27, no. 3 (September 1974): 500-519. Jose M. Vadi found a 50-50 split on this issue by barrio residents identifying themselves as "Mexicans." See his "Political Attitudes of Mexican Americans."

7. See John Staples Shockley, *Chicano Revolt in a Texas Town* (Notre Dame, Indiana: Notre Dame University Press, 1974), pp. 24-41.

8. Armando Rendon, *Chicano Manifesto* (New York: Macmillan, 1971) is a typical example of such writings. It must be emphasized that such generalizations permeate all the literature on Chicanos and American political life.

9. Clifton McCleskey and Bruce Merrill, "Mexican American Political Behavior in Texas," *Social Science Quarterly* 53, no. 4 (March 1973): 789-790.

10. *Majority-Minority Citizen Voter Attitudes*, p. 106.

11. Ibid.

12. Oral history interview with Congressman Edward Roybal conducted by Oscar J. Martinez, Director, Institute of Oral History, University of Texas at El Paso, October 23, 1975, Transcript #195, p. 10.

13. Fernando V. Padilla and Carlos B. Ramirez, "Patterns of Chicano Representation in California, Colorado and Nuevo Mexico," *Aztlan* 5, nos. 1 & 2 (Spring & Fall, 1974): 210-229.

14. Ibid., p. 209.

15. Ibid., pp. 197-198.

16. As reported by Tony Castro, *Dallas Morning News*, 26 December 1971: see also Richard Santillan, *La Raza Unida* (Los Angeles: Tiaquilo Publications, 1972), pp. 125-130.

17. Santillan, *La Raza Unida*, pp. 164-165; Art Wiene, "The Selling of The Senator, 1972," in *Practicing Texas Politics*, ed. Eugene W. Jones, Joe Risson, Lyle C. Brown, and Robert S. Trotter (Houghton Mifflin, 1974), p. 106.

18. Santillan, *La Raza Unida*, p. 36.

19. Ibid., p. 135.

Chicano Political Leadership:

"El que a dos amos sirve,
con uno queda mal."*

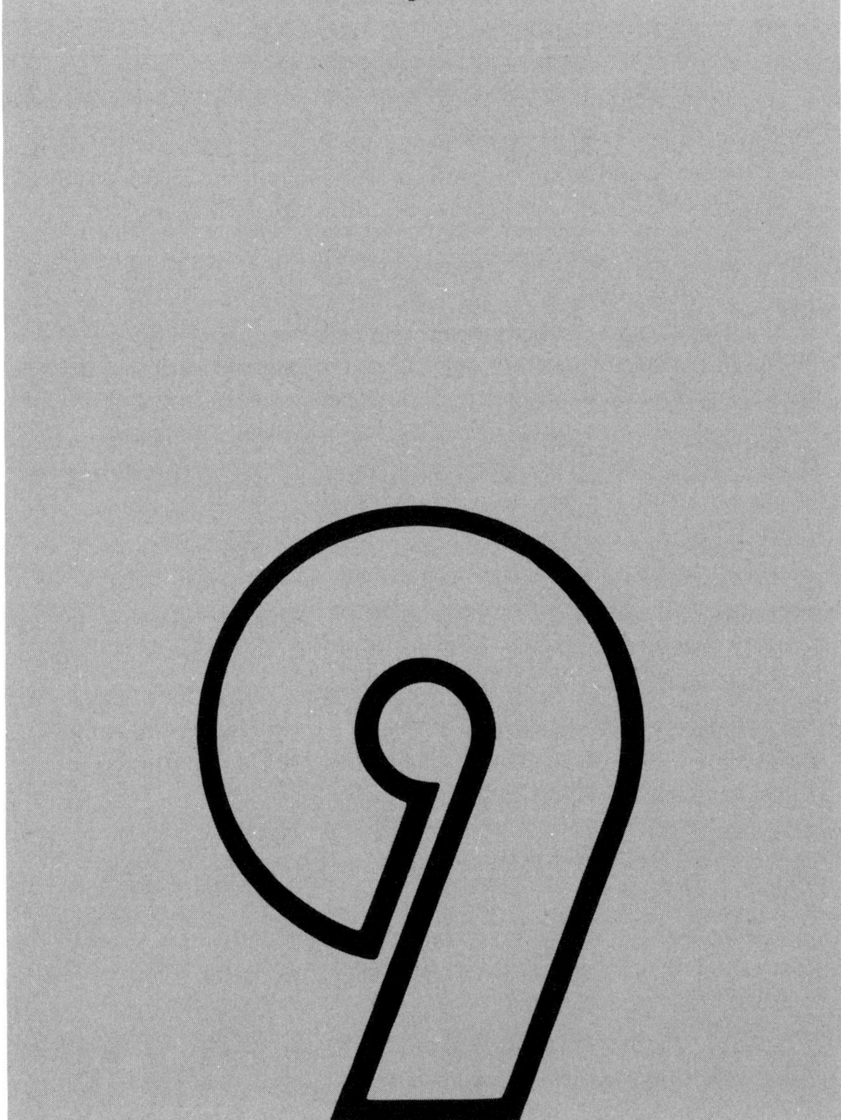

Leadership plays an essential role in the beginning of any political movement. Authentic and effective leadership reflects the demands of the masses and thus can mobilize a community and create within it organizations designed to achieve the community's objectives. As well as understanding and reflecting the community's present demands, authentic leaders also are able to anticipate demands. Therefore they are in a position to provide direction for political mobilization activities. Authentic leaders thus perform crucially important functions: it is they who articulate the often previously unspoken demands of the people, and it is they who carry those demands to decision makers.

Equally significant, however, are the leaders' symbolic functions. Often they serve as the focus of personal attachment; individuals identify with them and support the objectives of the movement through them. In such cases, a leader's individual charisma serves as the basis for mobilizing a previously unmobilized community.[1] It is through effective leadership, in other words, that oppressed communities can make best use of their scarce political resources. For these reasons, authentic and effective leadership is vital to the Chicano community.

The Myth and Reality of Chicano Leadership

Social scientists have long contended that Chicanos have been unable to develop effective political leadership. They attribute this "fact" to inherent cultural characteristics and support their argument with the value-laden and Anglo-biased generalizations which they use to describe Chicano culture generally. It is said, for example, that *envidia*, the innate jealousy which characterizes Chicano culture, keeps Chicanos from working together. Instead, it drives them to undercut any

*"He who tries to serve two masters will end up in trouble with one of them."

individual who begins to surface as a leader. Thus, there are no leaders in the barrio because there are no followers. Instead, all Chicanos consider themselves leaders.

An exactly contradictory stereotype also serves to explain the "lack of leadership" by claiming that Chicanos are so deferent to authority that they bind themselves to any leader who offers political or economic rewards. This unquestioning acceptance allows political bossess (*patrons* or *jefes politicos*) to manipulate Chicanos and prevents the development of authentic Chicano leaders. In a similar way, Chicanos are accused of succumbing to *personalismo*. Chicanos, like Latin Americans, need a strong personality with whom they can identify. Finding such a leader, Chicanos follow him devotedly and fanatically. Thus we see that the "lack of leadership" is attributed both to the fact that all Chicanos are leaders and will follow no one, and to the fact that Chicanos blindly attach themselves to political bosses and personalistic leaders.[2]

This "leadership vacuum," in fact, is a reflection of the biases with which researchers conducted their investigations. It is not indicative of the structure of the Mexican American community. Chicano communities, like all communities, have had a leadership structure that met and continues to meet the needs of the community to the extent that the dominant community allows it to function. The nature of the relationship between the dominant and Chicano communities has often defined and limited the Chicano leadership functions, however. To understand the development and role of Chicano leadership, therefore, it is necessary to study Chicano leadership within the context of this relationship. Ralph Guzman has developed a typology incorporating this requirement.[3] His typology identifies three types of leaders: the internal leader, the external leader, and the intermediary.[4]

Internal Leadership

Historically, many of the Chicanos who have served as community leaders have come from the middle class. Denied entry and success in the Anglo world, they focused their energies on the internal problems of the Chicano community. Such relatively affluent individuals as the grocer, small independent retailer, and barbershop proprietor have always served key functions. Because of their regular contact with members of the dominant community, they were looked to for advice and served as opinion leaders. Teachers and other professionals, to the extent that they existed, also served in these capacities. As "educated" members of the community they were recognized as possessing valuable political resources, including organizational skills and contacts with key members of the dominant community.

There are many other individuals who also have the respect and trust of the Chicano people on a neighborhood level who are often sought out for advice on personal as well as public problems. Such "reputational" leaders include many *women* in the community. Traditionally, the *Chicana* is a permanent resident in her community, knows the local situation very well, and interacts regularly with many of the community residents. In most barrios there are some respected *tias* ("aunts") or *doñas* ("older ladies"—a title of respect) who can be counted upon to assist in organizational activities as well as provide solutions for personal problems.

Such individuals are seldom visible to outsiders, but the contributions they make to the everyday life of the community are invaluable. It is they who help organize the community groups that meet the needs of the community when the institutions of the dominant society fail to do so. They are in every sense political leaders, but they have not been recognized as such because they function almost exclusively within their own communities.

External Leadership

Many of the key persons that influence and control the Chicano come from outside the community. These can be termed *external* leaders.

Problems and Benefits of External Leaders

According to the internal-colonial model, this is one of the major problems for Chicanos—that they are externally administered. Persons who play key roles in the Chicano community are representative not of the people but of the colonial powers. These people exploit the community resources for the benefit of external sources. However, external leadership need not necessarily stem from a colonial situation. In a pluralist society nonresidents of an area might play important roles in that community's affairs in a relationship of *mutual* benefit. Persons such as Fred Ross and Saul Alinsky, associated with the Los Angeles Community Service Organization (CSO), and William Higgs, who played a major role in Tijerina's Alianza activities, could be cited as examples of external leaders in Chicano political activities.

But outside leaders who come into the community may, even though honorably motivated, eventually begin to define the Chicanos' destiny for them. Much friction and conflict was produced in the black civil rights movement of the sixties, for example, when initially helpful external leaders, because of their resource advantage, eventually became not assistants and associates but leaders in every sense of the word.

Of course, external leaders can also be beneficial to the Chicano community in a pluralist society. They can, for example, provide services, resources, and skills which can help to lessen the immediate problems facing the community. Their assistance can be used in community organization as was the case with Ross and Alinsky. They can serve as valuable bridges between Chicanos and the outside world by providing Chicanos with a broadened perspective of the outside situation. Ideally, such external leaders would recruit and train Chicano leaders from the community, eventually working themselves out of a job. They would always remain in the background and work at keeping themselves in the role of staff rather than in executive leadership positions.

Types of External Leaders

An important type of external leader would be the Chicano who has left the barrio and "made it" in the Anglo society and then returns to help his less fortunate brothers and sisters in the barrio. With the gathering momentum of the Chicano movement, an increasing number of Chicanos are playing this role.

Among the most important of these external leaders are the several representatives of governmental agencies and the religious leaders with whom Chicanos deal regularly. These include social workers, labor leaders, and parish priests. Each of these is looked to as a source of information and advice. More significantly, each is also in a position to reward or punish at will. The social worker has a particularly key role because she usually has the power to determine a family's eligibility for participation in a given governmental welfare program. Social workers, then, function as interpreters of governmental regulations. It is not uncommon for Chicano families to become subservient to and dependent upon their case worker.

Priests function as external leaders because of the importance of the Catholic Church to the Mexican American people. Although the importance of the Church is diminishing, most Chicanos are still nominally Catholic, and they continue to show respect for the clergy. The role of the priest is enhanced because he is among the most educated persons in the barrio, and thus serves as a source of advice for both material and moral concerns.

Intermediary Leadership

The intermediate leader is perhaps the most significant of the three leadership types. Linking agents are necessary in Chicano politics because of the great difference in status and culture between the Chicano and Anglo people. The internal colonialism model need not necessarily be inferred from the fact that intermediate leaders are needed, but a strong case could be made for that position. Intermediaries would also exist in a pluralistic system, but in this case the gaps between the Chicano and Anglo group would be mainly cultural and not indicative of an inferior-superior relationship. It is often the case, however, that such representatives from the Chicano community are seen by the Anglo power structure as being intermediate in status. That is, they are perceived as somehow superior to the inferior Chicano masses that they represent and yet not quite up to their own Anglo standards.

Problems of the Intermediate Leader

Perhaps foremost is the problem of "dual validation." The intermediate leader has two constituencies, the Chicano community and Anglo society. More importantly, these constituencies are very dissimilar, often making irreconciliable demands upon him. He must be acceptable to both the Chicano population and the Anglo population—a task that is almost impossible in some situations. Because of the inequality of the two groups, the intermediate is often drawn into greater service towards the Anglo society. Sometimes the longer a person serves in this capacity, the more likely it is that he will lose touch with the group he is supposed to be interpreting to the controlling society.[5] These individuals consequently become less and less Chicano, or at least less and less representative of the Chicano. Others may succumb to the ego gratification of being in leadership positions. They begin to enjoy their status differentiation, their success and accomplishments, and to forget their origins and their mission. They often become defenders of that status quo of which they are becoming part.

Both of these occurrences can be termed *cooptation*, which is one of the major problems in the development of Chicano leadership.[6] The cooptation of native Chicano leaders drains the Chicano community of a great deal of leadership ability, a very valuable political resource. Such intermediaries may do more harm than good since their existence may prevent the recognition of authentic Chicano representatives. When they become more acceptable to the Anglo community because of their change, they are also more likely to be acceptable to the public decision makers than a new, if perhaps more representative, Chicano leader. The colonial model would explain that it is to be expected that only those Chicanos who are acceptable to the dominant Anglo society and whose values are similar to Anglo values will be accepted as intermediaries. This common occurrence leads to charges of *vendido* (sellout) or "tio tacoism" being made against many, if not all, Chicano political intermediaries.

Diminishing Importance of Intermediaries

Although intermediaries continue to occupy a central role in the Chicano leadership structure, changes in the Chicano community have diminished their importance, and the prospect is that their role will be even further diminished in future years. As more and more Chicanos become acculturated—that is, learn to deal with the system without becoming part of it, there will be an ever-decreasing need for intermediaries. As Chicanos become more educated, they will be able to cope with governmental representatives and officials without the aid of the intermediary, and their increased political awareness will make unnecessary the political role of these intermediaries. It is significant, moreover, that as Chicanos gain the political expertise to deal with the system, the community is showing an every-increasing willingness to trust and work with Mexican American professionals, the very professionals who several years earlier would have been accused of being *vendidos* and therefore not trustworthy.

Increased Participation by Professionals

This greater reliance on Chicano professionals is caused by several factors.

Stronger identification with community. First, Mexican American teachers, lawyers, and professionals in general are no longer afraid to identify with their community's causes. In years past such individuals jeopardized their professional futures if they identified with the Mexican American community. This was particularly true of educators, who had to prove to their Anglo superiors that they were "competent" and "objective,"—that they would reward only those Mexican American students who conformed to the Anglo model. Since Mexican American teachers had great difficulty getting jobs in past years, it is not surprising that, having been hired, they would have been reluctant to do anything that would risk their position. But recent investigations and court decisions have changed this, and today Chicano educators are often outspoken in defense of Chicano-oriented student activities. Thus, as these professionals have come out in favor of community issues, the community has begun to trust them more and more.

Need for expertise. The increased importance of Chicano professionals also reflects a change in the way in which Chicanos are attacking the problems confronting their community. The problems of housing, schooling, welfare rights, and police brutality are complex and not susceptible to simple solutions. Mexican Americans realize that perhaps the only way to "beat the system" is to use it; to do so they need the expertise of Chicano professionals. Bureaucrats and elected officials are able to dismiss the outraged charges of lower-class Mexican American laborers and housewives, but Chicano professionals force these officials to deal with the issues openly and directly. By being able to deal with these officials on their own terms, Chicano professionals make a significant contribution to the community and establish themselves as vital members of the group. As Chicano professionals continue to serve the community in this manner they help establish the conditions within which legitimate Chicano political leadership can develop, a leadership that will represent the community and serve its interests without being coopted by the rewards to which intermediaries sometimes succumb.

Obstacles to Chicano Leadership

The dilemma of Chicano political leadership will probably continue as long as Chicanos as a group remain in relatively powerless positions.

The Problem of Powerlessness

The ability to call public officials to account seems to follow power and power is still out of the Chicanos' hands. Authentic Chicano representation and leadership must be somehow dependent upon or responsible to the Chicano people. Responsibility and responsiveness depends upon sanctions, the authority to approve or disapprove, and in the United States sanctions are largely in Anglo hands. For example, even those few politicians who formally represent Chicano electoral majorities may ultimately depend upon non-Chicano financial resources, thus making it very risky for them to be truly representative of only their Chicano constituency. Another important consideration is that a Chicano leader, even one who is very responsive and sympathetic to the people, must operate within a given framework of institutions and processes which have been devised almost entirely without input from Chicanos. In other words, there are many Anglo institutional restraints which hinder an originally representative Chicano from continuing to act in that manner.

The Problem of Diversity

Another problem is posed by this question: *What* Chicano constituency does a Chicano leader represent? The Chicano people exhibit a tremendous diversity. There are intraethnic cleavages along regional, urban-rural, class, sex, and age lines. It would be very difficult for a national or even regional (that is, trans-state) political leader to enjoy support from all segments of the Chicano community. Middle-class Chicanos often cannot relate to some of the concerns of the working-class Chicanos. The current Chicano political movement is at least partly a working-class phenomenon, since many middle-class Chicanos have been coopted to some extent. Many have accommodated themselves to the values, norms and lifestyles of the Anglo, if they have not actually become part of that population. Traditionally, age has been a considerably important factor in determining leadership in the Mexican-American community—one who was older was more likely to gain respect. However, the current Chicano movement is largely a youth movement. Many of the important figures are young people, particularly students. This fact tends to again exaggerate or emphasize the leadership problem.

The problem of trust.

And finally, there are generally bad feelings attached to the whole notion of leadership in the Chicano community because in the past leadership has often been equated with selling out to the Anglo power structure or accommodating oneself to it. The price for leadership has too often been leaving behind one's *Chicanismo* or cultural characteristics and operating in the mode of the Anglo. Thus it is hard to convince the Chicano people that under altered political or socioeconomic circumstances there could emerge key persons who could retain their ties to the Chicano way of life and the Chicano people.

The seriousness of the problems generated by the often conflicting demands of distinct constituencies would seriously hamper even the best intentioned Chicano officials. Congressman Roybal thinks that the biggest obstacle to Chicano political advancement "has been the lack of unity.... Fighting for issues means unity, and you can't fight for an issue if there is disunity in your ranks... We still don't realize that we cannot divide our community five ways and expect to win. We have to be behind one candidate, behind one issue, behind on thing at a time. Once we have accomplished that, then we go to the next thing."[7]

Congressman de la Garza also considers this disunity to be a serious obstacle. "We don't have the unity that, for example, the blacks have, for many reasons. The main one, probably, is a question of geography because the Mexican American from California can be as different as black and white to the Mexican American from the Rio Grande valley in not even speaking the same dialect, as you call it. The same [is true for Mexican Americans] from Colorado, New Mexico, [and] Arizona. ... Because of your backgrounds, many times you desire different things."[8]

Raymond Telles, the first Mexican American mayor of El Paso, Texas, and currently a commissioner on the Equality Opportunity Commission in Washington, D.C., agrees. "Today, one of our problems is getting our different groups—all groups of Spanish-speaking ancestry—to unite. If they would unite, I think that they would have a better representation and better impact upon not only the political life but certainly the economic life of our people in the country."[9]

Chicano Constituencies and Leadership Styles

It should be now clear that the Chicano population is made up of varied groups and the Chicano experience, despite certain key common elements, is quite diverse. Therefore it is completely understandable why no one Chicano has emerged as a leader for the entire community. Unlike the blacks during the civil rights movement, Chicanos have no specific and easily identifiable target on which to focus. Thus, unlike the blacks, Chicanos, have not rallied around one individual or around one cause. Instead there have been several successful styles of leadership emerging across the Chicano community. Each of these styles reflects a specific view of Chicano-Anglo relations and appeals to a specific constituency.

The Style of Alienation

During the initial stages of the Chicano movement, the leaders who emerged then heavily emphasized rhetorical and emotional appeals to Mexicanness and cultural nationalism, combined with a willingness to use violence to attain their objectives and for self-defense. In part this rhetoric was patterned on the language of the black movement. In part, however, it also reflected the deep alienation and bitterness felt by many of the "*bato locos*" in the urban barrios. This belligerent and defiant stance appealed primarily to the alienated and most abused Chicanos in the urban centers. These "*batos*" are alienated from both the mainstream of Chicano society and Anglo society. Frustrated and angry at their situation, they were able to develop an identity and sense of pride and dignity through organizations that assaulted and defied the status quo. The Brown Berets typify this type of organization, and Rodolfo "Corky" Gonzáles of Denver's Crusade for Justice epitomizes this leadership style. Although highly publicized, this style appeals to a relatively small constituency within the barrio.[10]

The Moral Crusader[11]

An equally oppressed but perhaps less alienated constituency is the migrant farm worker. Like the *bato loco,* the migrant farm worker is impoverished; unlike the *bato loco*, however, the migrant farm worker is well within the mainstream of Chicano society. As a group, they are among the most "Mexican," or traditional, of the Chicanos, and from any educational and social perspective, they are among the most oppressed.

The leadership style that has had the greatest appeal among the farm workers is that of the "moral crusader." Outraged at the injustices suffered by his people, the moral crusader appeals to both the farm worker and to citizens of good will across the nation to join together to help create a better world. César Chávez is the best example of this approach. Because of his commitment to moral principles, militants often accuse Chávez of being naive. Chávez, like Martin Luther King before him, however, understands the realities of American political life, and his commitment to principle makes him a tireless and unyielding defender of the cause rather than an incompetent and easily maneuvered idealist. Farm workers, the most publicized of Chicanos constituencies, clearly enjoy more support among the dominant community than does any other Chicano group. Nonetheless, the migrants also represent only a small portion of the Mexican American people.

A third constituency that also represents a traditional and small segment of the Chicano population are the Hispanos of northern New Mexico. An agriculturally based people deeply committed to traditional values, Hispanos have a strong sense of identity and community. A century of legal and illegal maneuvers has alienated their lands from them, yet they remain completely committed to their rural lifestyle and their lands. Reies López Tijerina mobilized this sector with appeals resembling that of the moral crusader. But he combined his cries of moral outrage with a commitment to direct action and a willingness to resort to force to reclaim communal lands. Defeated in his initial efforts, López Tijerina has recently followed more closely the "moral crusade" approach. This is evidenced by the Brotherhood Awareness Crusade he now heads which emphasizes love, cooperation, and understanding among all people.

The Alienated Reformer

A fourth constituency responds to the appeal of the "alienated reformer." In socioeconomic terms, this group may be described as including primarily members of the lower class and lower middle class. Relative to the *batos locos* and migrant workers, they enjoy a semblance of economic security. They include the unskilled urban worker and many of the poor farmers in the rural communities of Texas, Arizona, and California. Unlike the *batos*, they have a sense of community and typify the mainstream of the Mexican American people. They too, however, are alienated and frustrated by their lack of opportunity, and they are organizing to overcome their situation.

The "alienated reformer" has mobilized this constituency through appeals to group consciousness and cultural solidarity. Despite these rhetorical and emotional appeals, "alienated reformers" are extremely pragmatic and utilize whatever means are available to achieve their ends. Thus, when possible, they use the electoral machinery. Direct confrontation and verbal attacks are also employed, as are negotiations with the bureaucracies at all levels of government. The distinguishing characteristics of the "alienated reformer" are that his approach is entirely Chicano-oriented and utilizes the system to achieve its end. The objective is Chicano control of decision-making machinery. Although several examples of this style can be found across the Southwest, the best known and most successful—indeed, one of the initiators—is José Angel Gutiérrez. The organization and takeover of Crystal City which he led has become a model for Chicano activists everywhere. This leadership style is becoming increasingly important in the Chicano community, as is suggested by the fact that its constituency makes up the largest segment of the Chicano community.

The Style of Accommodation

Finally, the constituency which has historically produced the fewest authentic leaders but which should have produced the most is the Chicano middle class. Composed primarily of skilled laborers, craftsmen, white-collar employees, and a few college-trained professionals, most of whom are teachers, this sector enjoys relative economic security and acceptance by the dominant society. It is from this sector that the LULAC emerged in the 1920s. Until very recently, few changes were seen in its political style. Its leaders were those most adept at dealing with the dominant system as bargainers committed to working within the system. These leaders were convinced that only by participating in mainstream politics could Chicanos derive any benefits from the dominant society. Representative of this group are Senator Joseph Montoya of New Mexico, Congressmen Henry B. González and Eligio de la Garza of Texas, and Governor Raul Castro of Arizona.

Because of their pragmatic and cautious approach, none of these men can be considered a leader of the majority Chicano community.

To many, they are at best misguided, at worst *vendidos*. Chicano activists bitterly oppose both Texas congressmen, and Congressman González has publicly attacked the activists.[12] In California, the MAPA and the Mexican American Unity Council refused to endorse Edward Roybal in his bid for reelection in 1970.[13] The Arizona branch of the United Farmworkers Union bitterly attacks Governor Castro. In sum, none of these men can rally the entire Chicano community to their support.

The New Middle-Class Leader

Recently, however, the Chicano middle class has begun to produce a new type of leader who combines a willingness to work within the system with a commitment to Chicano causes and an identification with Chicano issues. Examples of such individuals include former Lieutenant Governor Roberto Mondragón of New Mexico, State Representative and Speaker of the House Rubén Valdez of Colorado, Governor Jerry Apodaca of New Mexico, and State Senator and Majority Leader Alfredo Gutierrez of Arizona. Through their commitment to Chicano causes, such men are awakening in the middle-class Chicano the realization that the problems of the poor are also their concern. They seem also to be convincing the militant Chicano that they can be trusted and are not *vendidos*. In sum, this new leadership seems to have the potential to unite the Chicano community as it has never been united.[14] As of today, however, this potential is far from realized.

The possible contribution of this new leadership and constituency cannot be overstated. The middle-class Chicano has the resources necessary to engage in and support Chicano political activity. As long as those resources remain unmobilized, the Chicano community will have to rely greatly on the dominant society for assistance, and that assistance will in all likelihood be given only under specified conditions. If these resources are mobilized, however, it is the Chicano community that will be able to demand concessions from the dominant society. This new leadership, then, is in a position to mobilize and utilize Chicano resources as they have never been before.

As would be expected, the Chicano community has produced leaders reflective of its various experiences. To date, no one can be identified as *the* Chicano leader just as no one Chicano can be considered the "typical" Chicano. So long as variations in the conditions and experiences of the Chicano exist from region to region, the movement will require a diversity of leadership and styles and tactics.[15] Nonetheless, it does seem clear that there is a dire need for a consensus on an overarching common objective around which all leaders and constituencies would unite. Until such a consensus is forged, the Chicano movement will remain fragmented and sporadic.

Chicano Leadership: Three Explanations

The elitist and colonial models of American politics seem to explain a great deal of the development of Chicano leadership styles. Both models would expect that Chicano leaders who challenge the system be either coopted or eliminated. Historically, those who did not accommodate were in fact eliminated. This continues to be the case, argue the militants. In Los Angeles, police infiltrated and harassed the Brown Berets until they effectively broke up that organization. The police murdered Rubén Salazar and numerous Crusade for Justice activists. They harassed, arrested, and brutalized Reies Tijerina and his family until he was defeated and immobilized. All of these men threatened the very basis of political and economic domination and, since they would not be compromised, they were broken or eliminated.

The colonial model also explains why the middle class has been unable to produce vigorous and dynamic leadership. First, to insure that Chicanos believe that they in fact have representation, Chicanos are allowed to hold major office. However, those Chicanos who attain these positions are in fact dependent on the dominant community and not on Chicano constituencies. Thus they in no way represent the Mexican American people. Like the tribal chieftains in the English and French colonies, such Chicano officials legitimize rather than challenge their subordination.

Although both of these models describe the Chicano historically, it is the pluralistic analysis that best accommodates recent changes in the Chicano leadership structure. Chicano leaders such as César Chávez and Governor Apodaca illustrate that the system has opened itself to effective Chicano leadership. These and other men advocate Chicano causes against strong Anglo opposition, and they do so successfully. Where once they might have been eliminated, now they exercise their rights as freely as does any Anglo politician. Moreover, even activists such as Corky Gonzáles and José Angel Gutiérrez carry on their activities openly. The pluralists would argue that the Crusade is harassed only when it violates the law; José Angel Gutiérrez is so successful that now it is he who can harass the Anglo.

It could, of course, be argued that none of these examples poses a real threat to the dominant community. The Crusade is isolated; Gutiérrez's activities are restricted to a small part of South Texas; incumbent politicians by definition are a part of and support the system. While such arguments are correct, they grossly underestimate the contributions that each of these leaders makes to the Chicano community. As will be shown in the next chapter, each of these stands as a change model within the Chicano community, and therefore each is greatly significant. It might also be suggested that the only reason such leaders are not eliminated is because they are too important. Such an argument underestimates the destructive capacity of the dominant system, as the examples of Martin Luther King, the Black Panther leaders in Detroit and Chicago, and others painfully illustrate.

In sum, then, it seems that effective Chicano leadership is developing. It may be too soon to determine if those leaders will be allowed to change substantially the conditions that affect the Chicano. If they are not, then the elitist and colonial analysis will have been accurate. If they are, then clearly this would indicate that the system has evolved toward a more pluralistic structure.

Chapter 9
Notes

1. Max Weber, *The Theory of Social and Economic Organization* (New York: The Free Press, 1947).

2. For example John R. Martínez, "Leadership and Politics," in *La Raza: Forgotten Americans*, ed. Julian Samora (Notre Dame, Indiana: University of Notre Dame Press, 1966); Paul M. Sheldon, "Community Participation and the Emerging Middle Class," in *La Raza: Forgotten Americans*, ed. Samora.

3. Ralph Guzmán, "The Political Socialization of the Mexican American People" (Ph.D. dissertation, University of California, Los Angeles, 1969), pp. 282-336.

4. This typology is also employed in the discussion of leadership in Leo Grebler, Joan W. Moore, and Ralph Guzmán, *The Mexican American People* (New York: The Free Press, 1970), pp. 548-554.

5. Statement by Rep. Dawson of Chicago.

6. The operation of cooptation is listed as a problem in the development of Chicano leadership by James B. Watson and Julian Samora, "Subordinate Leadership in a Bicultural Community: An Analysis," *American Sociological Review* 19 (1954): 419-420.

7. Oral interview with Congressman Edward Roybal conducted by Oscar J. Martinez, Director, Institute of Oral History, University of Texas at El Paso, October 23, 1975, transcript #195, pp. 15-16.

8. Oral interview with Congressman Eligio de la Garza conducted by Oscar J. Martinez, Director, Institute of Oral History, University of Texas at El Paso, October 22, 1975, transcript #218, p. 16.

9. Oral interview with Raymond Telles conducted by Oscar J. Martinez, Director, Institute of Oral History, University of Texas at El Paso, October 22, 1975, transcript #193, p. 9.

10. Rodolfo Acuña, *Occupied America* (San Francisco: Canfield Press, 1972) and Rona Marcia Fields Fox, "The Brown Berets: A Participant Observation Study of Social Action in the Schools of Los Angeles, (Ph.D. dissertation, University of Southern California, Los Angeles, 1970).

11. This term was developed by Charles Hamilton, black political scientist at Columbia University and coauthor of *Black Power*.

12. Henry B. González, "The Hate Issue" *Congressional Record*, April 22, 1969, vol. 115, pp. 9951-54.

13. Richard Santillan, *La Raza Unida* (Los Angeles: Tlaquilo Publication, 1973).

14. Biliana C. S. Ambrecht found in her study of the leadership of community organizations that a new core of authentic, representative, and committed Chicano leaders are emerging among some middle-class groups. See her *Politicizing the Poor: The Legacy of the War on Poverty in a Mexican American Community* (New York: Praeger, 1976).

15. Armando Rendón calls for a variety of *revolucionarios* (revolutionaries)—a leadership core of diverse backgrounds, methods, motivations, and styles —*Chicano Manifesto* (New York: Macmillan, 1971), p. 108.

Political Change Strategies:

"Con deseos no se hacen templos."*

Thus far we have described the position of Chicanos in the American political process. Reviewing that material suggests a number of conclusions. First, there can be no denying that historically American society has utilized schools, law enforcement agencies, economic structures, political institutions, and violence to exploit and oppress the Chicano. A second generalization is that Chicanos have responded to that oppression in a variety of ways.

What is significant to us is the resiliency Chicanos have shown in this struggle. Despite the widespread violence of the early years and the sometimes more subtle abuses combined with violent outbursts in recent years, the Chicano people have persevered in their efforts to attain equality and maintain their cultural identity. It is also clear that over the last decade Chicanos showed themselves unwilling to wait patiently for improvement on the terms dictated by the dominant culture. Finally, it can not be denied that Chicanos have made some gains in recent years, although the significance and permanence of those gains is yet to be determined.

Our purpose in this chapter is to review some strategies and tactics that certain segments of the Chicano community have developed recently. We intend both to evaluate their degree of success and to suggest the importance of these examples to other Chicano communities. We have chosen to omit an analysis of the best known effort of Chicanos to better their condition—that of César Chávez and the farm worker—because it is more a special case of a conventional political strategy than a new form of change strategy. Chávez has long been committed to working within the existing political structures and his efforts have been to establish solid coalitions with Anglo politicians who will help him attain his ends. Thus he chose not to attend the 1972 Raza Unida convention. For these reasons many Chicano militants question Chávez's validity as a Chicano spokesman. "We're not castigating Chávez nor saying we don't support his move-

*"With wishes no temples are built."

ment. We are saying that we have serious disagreements on how things are going to be accomplished . . . . I understand he is motivated the way he is, but there are a lot of Chicanos who can't see it and are even being turned off by Chávez."[1] Because of these disagreements, even if Chávez had attended the 1972 convention he probably would not have been allowed to speak.

While we do not agree with this indictment, we understand the reasoning behind it. To many, Chávez is primarily a labor leader, and he saw himself as such at the beginning of his efforts. Some argue therefore that he became a Chicano leader by default. Nonetheless, it must be recognized that Chávez is a central figure in the Movement as it is defined by Hernandez.[2] Indeed, when asked to respond to the accusations by militants that Chávez was not a Chicano leader, Dolores Huerta, executive vice president of the United Farm Workers, heatedly responded: "They're full of crap. Without Chávez there would not have been a Chicano movement."[3]

Whichever assessment is correct is beside the point. What is clear is that because of his approach a significant number of Chicanos do not consider Chávez representative of the Chicano movement, regardless of his self-perception. The activities we will describe are directed by individuals, including a few Anglos, who see themselves as committed to the Movement, who organized to serve a Chicano constituency, and who reject in practice if not in principle conventional coalition politics.

La Raza Unida

Among the most controversial, publicized, and significant developments of the Chicano movement is La Raza Unida Party (LRUP). It is difficult to date precisely when and where Raza Unida began. Some scholars suggest its birth was in Texas, although it is also possible to argue that Raza Unida had its beginning in Colorado in 1968 with the first Chicano National Youth Congress.[4] Whatever its date of origin, what is of greater concern is the meaning it has had for the Chicano movement—its objectives, its successes, and its future.

Significance of Raza Unida

Raza Unida indicated, above all, that Chicanos were no longer willing to support either of the dominant political parties since both have maintained the political and socioeconomic system that continues to exclude Chicanos from key positions. Chicano militants described the party system as a two-headed snake, with neither head genuinely responsive to or concerned with Chicanos.[5] For years Chicanos had supported the Democratic party as the lesser of two evils, but to the militants such a strategy was no longer satisfying. By developing their own party, Chicano leaders hoped to achieve two immediate ends. First, they hoped to show Anglo politicians that Chicanos were no longer dependent on them. Second, they desired to make the Chicano community aware of the possibilities to make changes and improve their conditions through the development and use of alternative strategies.

Thus, Raza Unida began not merely as a political party but as "an ethnic institution that will break the cycle of Chicano repression by a variety of organizational efforts. Raza Unida is not a vehicle for entering the mainstream of United States society but is a safeguard for the Mexican American bilingual-bicultural uniqueness."[6] Raza Unida leaders consequently directed their efforts toward long-term goals built on the foundation of a unified Chicano community rather than toward immediate electoral victories. In fact, such electoral triumphs were almost irrelevant to some Chicano leaders such as Corky Gonzales.

Characteristics of Raza Unida Branches

The idea of a Chicano political party spread rapidly across the Southwest, and activists throughout the area began forming Raza Unida branches. Wherever they were formed, these parties shared certain characteristics. Above all, they explicitly rejected any cooperation with the traditional parties and with any individual working with those parties. The Sacramento party constitution states:

> This party is being formed as an alternative to the traditional stronghold the Democratic and Republican parties have on the United States political system. The Raza people recognize that these two parties have ignored the existing problems of the brown minority and in many cases have exploited them for their own advantage. Unifying the brown minorities will be the key factor for La Raza Unida.[7]

In San Fernando, California, Raza Unida states: "La Raza Unida party through its candidates and its platform getting on the November general election ballots, shall have the power to deny our votes to the lesser of two evils candidates and parties of the Anglo establishment–Democratic and Republican party–by running our own candidates on our own platform."[8] The Tucson branch states: "La Raza Unida Party will not support any candidate of the Democratic, Republican party or an individual who supports these parties."[9] The Colorado branch makes a comparable declaration: "We re-affirm and re-state our position as an independent political party, making independent decisions and not as an endorsing organization."[10] The Texas branch articulates perhaps best of all the need for a Chicano party. "Significant change from within the two-party system will never come about. Change in a corrupt system can never happen because those who profess to institute change are the very same who corrupted that system in the first place."[11]

In California and Arizona, the Raza Unida parties carried this separation to its logical conclusion by restricting their membership to fellow Latin Americans. Both the California and Tucson chapters state in their platforms:

> Any person of La Raza registered in La Raza and/or works actively to support the program and activities of the party will be considered a member with the right to participate in all decision-making process of the party on the basis of one person and one vote. By "La Raza" we mean those people who are descendants of or come from Mexico, Central America, South America and Antilles.[12]

Because the various LRUP chapters agree on the need to politicize the Chicano community around key issues, they all tend to stress the same issues.[13] There are, however, differences among the several chapters. Within California, the Northern California chapter outlines a foreign policy, while the southern California chapter does not. The southern California chapter also is more restrictive in its definition of *Raza*, limiting its membership exclusively to Chicanos. Northern California includes all Latin Americans as *Raza*.[14]

Degrees of Success

The strategies and tactics employed by all the chapters have also been similar. All have tried to use the common bond of culture to mobilize the Chicano community and convert that unity into a political resource. The specific successes that each branch might have had in mobilizing barrios to deal with specific local issues are not easily documented. What is clear, however, is that even if such successes have been realized, they have not resulted in a sustained mobilization or unity. In other words, the Chicano community has not responded to the efforts of Raza Unida as the party leaders expected.

Colorado. In Denver, for example, the Crusade for Justice, headquarters for Colorado's Raza Unida, was initially very successful in awakening the Chicano population to the issues of police brutality and educational discrimination. By the 1970s, however, the Crusade began to be increasingly isolated from the majority of the barrio people. Now it is not a significant factor in barrio mobilization. On the other hand, the Crusade has been extremely successful in organizing its own school and in developing cultural programs to regain and maintain ethnic identity. Thus from a conventional perspective, it would seem that the Crusade is not very successful. From the perspective of establishing an autonomous ethnic institution, however, there is no doubt that the Crusade is doing well.

Arizona. A similar pattern characterizes the development of Raza Unida in Tucson. Led by Sal Baldenegro and others, Raza Unida initially began as a consciousness-raising group. Meetings were held to discuss the need for a party and how that party might be organized. All agreed that the party would not be primarily concerned with electoral politics until an effective mass base had been established. That base could be established only by proving to the community that Raza Unida, unlike the Democrats who dominated the barrio, was more interested in serving the people than in winning their votes.

For several years, therefore, Raza Unida functioned as a pressure group and community organizer. Members devoted themselves to working on barrio causes ranging from demands for educational reform to the building of parks and other facilities for barrio use. They first ventured into the political arena in 1972 only to have their candidate for city councilman overwhelmingly defeated. Ironically, he received the majority of his support in non-Chicano areas. In 1974, however, Raza Unida's candidate to the school board was elected, whether by Chicano or Anglo votes is unclear. One similarity between the Denver and Tucson efforts, then, is that both have failed to mobilize widespread Chicano support despite their commitment to the Chicano cause.

California. However unsuccessful the Arizona and Colorado Raza Unida efforts are by conventional standards, they are more developed than comparable groups in California. The major factor keeping the California chapters alive is the "statistical pressure of formidable

Chicano political power in California."[15] Chicano militants realize that if mobilized, Chicanos would be in a position to force either dominant party to deal with them. Yet they have been unable to mobilize the community, for a variety of reasons.

A major factor preventing the success of Raza Unida in California is the lack of effective leadership. In Arizona and Texas, college-educated youth have played key roles in Raza Unida. In both of these cases this leadership group has been able to benefit from the experience of university life without separating themselves from their community. In California, however, this group acts more as "enlightened elites" than as fellow Chicanos.[16] On the other hand, the hard-core membership of the party in California is recruited from the ranks of the *bato loco*, the Chicano street dude. In combination, these two groups have alienated many would-be and former Raza Unida supporters.[17]

New Mexico. In this state LRUP has fared poorly. Perhaps the major obstacle in this state is the cooptation of most politicized Chicanos into the ranks of the Democratic, and to a lesser extent the Republican, parties. Most of the state's Chicanos have a long-term identification with the Democratic party, and indeed a large proportion of the state's public office holders are Chicanos.[18] One former state Democratic chairman, a Chicano, stated in a confidential conversation with the author, "We don't need a Raza Unida party for Chicanos in New Mexico because we already have one—the Democratic party."

In New Mexico LRUP has attained some success only in areas of the most militant and factionalist politics, as in Las Vegas, or in areas where Chicanos have heretofore been excluded from conventional political participation, as in the southeastern area of the state. On the other hand as in Democratic machine-dominated Rio Arriba County, Raza Unida has generally served as a forceful reminder to the major parties that there exists some serious dissatisfaction with their service to the Chicano masses of New Mexico.

Nonconventional successes. If measured in conventional terms, such as electoral triumph, Raza Unida in California, Arizona, New Mexico, and Colorado has been a failure. In terms of educating the public or at least raising issues concerning the welfare of the Chicano community, however, Raza Unida groups have fared better. When measured against this standard, Raza Unida in Colorado has done quite well. Above all, the Crusade for Justice stands as an example of an autonomous Chicano organization that has survived despite the lack of widespread support or financial assistance from the Anglo community.[19] More importantly, Corky Gonzáles is respected for his strongly independent stance. Even Chicano leaders who disagree with the extreme militance and separatist position of the Crusade acknowledge that Corky stands alone as a Chicano leader who has been unwilling to compromise his position and accept financial support from Anglo politicians.[20]

Texas. When compared to these organizations, Raza Unida in Texas has been extremely successful. Organizationally, it is far more developed than any other branch and has enjoyed much greater electoral success than any other contingent. Its educational efforts have also been far more effective than those of Raza Unida parties elsewhere. Measured by both internal and external criteria, then, La Raza Unida Party of Texas is the only Raza Unida chapter that is achieving its objectives. To understand the full implications of Raza Unida for both the Chicano community and the nation in general, it is necessary to understand the factors contributing to the party's success in Texas.

MAYO and MAUC

As is true in the classic colonial model, the origins of Raza Unida and the politics of "liberation" in Texas can be traced to the activities of several individuals, some of whom had benefited most from the "colonial" system. These well-educated, articulate, and acculturated students could easily have become coopted leaders with secure positions within established structures. Instead, they took advantage of their privileged position to analyze why they had "made it" while others had failed.[21]

Founding of MAYO

This analysis and discussion led to the founding of the Mexican American Youth Organization (MAYO) at St. Mary's University in San Antonio in 1967. Its initial leadership included José Angel Gutiérrez, Carlos Guerra, Mario Campean, and Willie Velasquez. Others who soon joined the group were Juan Patlan and Ernie Cortez. Charles Cotrell, a political scientist at St. Mary's, worked closely with this group and undoubtedly influenced its initial direction.[22]

This context and leadership group was to become the core of Chicano activism in Texas for the next decade. From this group would come not only Raza Unida leaders, but the key figures in Chicano politics in San Antonio and across the South Texas Valley. MAYO, in other words, was more than the beginning of the Chicano takeover in Crystal City. It was the beginning of a new style and intensity of Chicano politics that would have an impact on all levels of the Chicano community.[23]

Founding of MAUC

The MAYO leadership recognized the need to broaden their base and work with all of the Mexican American community. To this end they founded the Mexican American Unity Council (MAUC). In many ways MAUC was only a front for MAYO. Both organizations committed themselves to openly confronting the dominant society and challenging existing political relationships. Initially, MAUC had little impact, but this changed in 1968 when the Ford Foundation began to fund its activities. At this point, the paper distinction between MAYO and MAUC became a key difference. So long as MAUC did not become overtly involved in politics, it was eligible for this funding. Since MAUC and MAYO had almost identical memberships, the distinction between the two became crucial if deceptive. MAUC would commit its energies to community organization and self-help projects, and MAYO would take up the political responsibilities.

Successes of MAYO and MAUC

For a time this nominal division achieved its end. MAUC and MAYO enjoyed increasing success in their activities. Key victories included the elimination of the no-Spanish rule then prevalent in San Antonio schools. This goal was achieved as a result of the activities of the Edgewood Concerned Parents, a Chicano parents' organization which MAUC helped organize and fund. Mario Campean then ran for mayor and almost forced a runoff election. In the closed San Antonio electoral system, to have a Mexican American challenge the decision makers so openly was unthinkable; to have a radical Chicano activist almost defeat the establishment's candidate was intolerable. This narrow victory forced the city's elite to respond to MAUC and MAYO, and their response led to the end of the first stage of Chicano militant activities. However, it also led directly to a second and ultimately more successful stage.

Reaction to MAYO and MAUC

That MAUC and MAYO frightened and angered the Anglo community was to be expected. That, indeed, was part of their objective. More significant, however, was that they angered Congressman Henry B. González, and it was he who brought institutional power down on these organizations. By 1969, MAUC's strength was broken. Patlan and others believe that they were put under police surveillance and that their phones were tapped. Congressman González made his anger known on the floor of the House of Representatives, where he openly attacked MAYO.[24] He also used his position as a member of the Banking and Currency Committee to help pass into law the 1969 Tax Reform Act, which was partly aimed at preventing foundations from funding groups such as MAUC/MAYO. The legislation achieved its aim, and MAUC/MAYO became relatively inactive.

The Crystal City Takeover

While learning from the San Antonio experience, several of the MAYO/MAUC leaders, spearheaded by José Angel Gutiérrez, began developing the Winter Garden project. Gutiérrez realized that he could beat the system by using it. That is, he knew that the electoral mechanisms which had been used so devastatingly against Chicanos could be captured by Chicanos and used to their own advantage. All they needed was organization and numbers. In San Antonio they learned how to organize; the Winter Garden area in South Texas provided the numbers.

Gutiérrez mobilized the Chicanos around discriminatory policies in the schools. This was an issue with which the entire community could identify. The protest against these policies led to the community mobilizing for and winning the next school board elections. This triumph led to even more extensive politicization and Chicanos soon took over all elected positions in the city. The culmination of Gutiérrez's efforts came when he was elected judge of Zavala County in 1974.

Motivation for the Takeover

The takeover engineered by Gutiérrez in Crystal City has been well described elsewhere.[25] What is important to add here is the motivation for these events. Most significantly, to understand the Crystal City takeover it is necessary to understand that individual and institutional racism have been a primary and every-present factor in southern Texas politics for over a century. The MAYO/MAUC leaders suffered under it, realized its depth and were able to turn it against Anglo politicians. Chicanos throughout the area, including the politically conservative, reveal even in casual conversations a bitter and deep resentment against the *gringo*, and Gutiérrez tapped this bitterness and converted it into a political resource.

For this reason the Crystal City takeover cannot be construed as merely a political victory. It was and is far more than that, and Gutiérrez and others do their best to insure that the community understands this greater meaning. It was above all a move toward freedom, toward the right to be *Mexicano*, to speak Spanish, to attend school, to live with dignity. It was not, therefore, a simple political contest but instead a battle by Chicanos to overthrow their oppressors. Both sides knew this, and both sides did their best to win.

Knowing he had a constituency and the necessary numbers Gutiérrez committed himself to mobilizing around *Chicanismo*. His success documents better than anything else the depth of Chicano resentment toward Anglos in that part of Texas. Gutiérrez also described the meaning of the battle to the Anglo.

> The opposition. All of the Gringos and the coopted Chicanos in the county. The election judges, the tally clerks, the sheriff, his deputies, Texas Rangers, the highway patrol, the road department, the Del Monte plant, ranchers, store owners, farmers. They're fighting like tigers with their backs to the wall. If we win sheriff, they've lost their guns.[26]

Factors Supporting the Takeover

José Ángel's extraordinary success was the result of several factors. There is no question that "outside" support was valuable, or that he is himself an extraordinarily capable organizer. But other communities have received outside support, and capable leadership exists in all Chicano communities.[27] In addition to these were other conditions which may be less common to other areas. First, there was the sheer mass of numbers sufficient to completely take over. Second, the interaction among these masses reinforced the sense of identity, recognition of exploitation and oppression, and the consequent willingness to support an effort to overthrow that oppressive system.[28] Third, the objective conditions convinced the masses that they had little to lose even if their efforts failed, and they believed that they would not fail.

Impact of the Takeover

Although the specific achievements of the Chicano takeover have been documented elsewhere, it is perhaps useful here to reiterate the psychological and long-term implications of these changes.[29] More significant than the initiation of bilingual programs is that Chicanos no longer are made to feel ashamed of being Chicano. More important than having Chicanos in office is that these Chicano officials are responsible to the community. Major issues are openly discussed and acted upon at public meetings which, as José Angel states, are "just as easily seen as replicas of a New England town meeting or a Communist Party Central Committee."[30] Chicanos never participated so directly in public life before, and they will be unlikely to give up their newly gained power to anyone in the future.

The impact of Crystal City has also been felt outside of Texas. In Parlier, California, Chicanos found themselves in comparable conditions and achieved a comparable takeover.[31] The battle there was won more quickly, but the results were the same. Chicanos began immediately replacing the dominant Anglos with Chicanos, and the image of the city changed as radically as it had in Crystal City. The Parlier example is particularly noteworthy in view of the fact that scholars had suggested that the Crystal City experience could not be repeated elsewhere.[32] Comparable efforts are also under way in Robstown, Mathis, and elsewhere in Texas.[33]

Problems from the Takeover

The Crystal City triumph generated a completely new set of problems for the community.[34] Economically, the city has a tenuous future. No new industry has been attracted to the city since the takeover, and the tax base has been severely affected by the loss of 500 Anglo families who have left the city.[35] There is also evidence suggesting that Raza Unida leaders tolerate no opposition. Gutiérrez himself admits to intimidating tactics, and he justifies this on the ground that at their present stage of development the programs are not strong enough to withstand continuous infighting. As one key member of Raza Unida stated, "Democracy is bullshit at the beginning." In the schools, there appears to be a tendency to deemphasize academics to the point that the more academically advanced students are being ignored or not challenged and student expectations are lower. This may be a temporary development aimed at correcting the feelings of failure which the schools formerly instilled in Chicano students.

Statewide Effort in Texas

The Crystal City experience is but one side of the activities of Raza Unida in Texas. The other side is the statewide party effort. The difference between the two is great, and each offers significant insights into strategies for other Chicano communities.

Decision for Statewide Effort

After the initial although brief success in San Antonio and the more important triumph in Crystal City, Raza Unida leaders decided to make their effort statewide. Gutiérrez strongly opposed this decision, arguing for continued local mobilization leading to the piecemeal takeover of South Texas and other communities across the state with large Chicano populations. Not only were such victories within their grasp, but the cumulative power of such triumphs would make Raza Unida a formidable force in state and thus national politics. But in October 1971, Raza Unida leaders decided to participate in 1972 statewide elections. Gutiérrez, despite his disagreement with this strategy, threw his impressive energies and influence into the campaign.

Raza Unida leaders immediately confronted the problem of what races they would contest and who their candidates would be. Initially the hope was that leading Chicano Democrats such as Joe Bernal would run as Raza Unida. After an exhaustive effort failed to recruit any "name" candidates, Raza Unida turned to Ramsey Muniz. Muniz had worked with Raza Unida since 1968, and he was selected to run as the party's nominee for governor only because there was no one else.[36]

The 1972 Election

Unlike the tactics of its California or Arizona counterparts, the Texas Raza Unida efforts to elect Muniz in 1972 were characterized by pragmatic coalition politics.

Broad-based appeal. Muniz ran a "poor people's" campaign rather than a Chicano campaign. "Raza Unida is not just a party for the Mexicanos. We welcome the Black and White, Japanese Americans, Chinese Americans, poor people, liberals, anybody who wants a change. We don't judge people by the color of their skin. We judge them by their behavior. And the Republicans and Democrats have misbehaved for years."[37] This broad-based appeal is reflected in the Texas party's platform, which was extremely similar to both the Texas Democratic party's platform and the national Democratic platform.[38] Moreover, Raza Unida ran whites and blacks for local office in Texas and was endorsed by Ralph Abernathy of the Southern Christian Leadership Conference.[39]

Reasons for failure. Although Muniz did much better than had been expected by winning 6.2 percent of the vote statewide, the broad-based appeal failed. In part, this may have been a result of Muniz's inexperience and apparent lack of preparation for the statewide office.[40] It also proved once again what Gutiérrez and others had been stating for years: white liberals preferred to vote for a conservative Anglo Democrat rather than a liberal Chicano who agreed with them on most if not all the key issues. "Muniz is espousing almost exactly the same platform Farenthold ran on. Yet Sissy (Farenthold) is supporting Dolph Briscoe who she has described as a 'bowl of pablum.' "[41] Muniz and the party thus incurred the wrath of these liberals by asking their supporters to abstain from the Democratic party primary in which Farenthold sought to win the nomination from Dolph Briscoe. She lost the primary, and the white liberal reaction was bitter: "The best chance, the only chance this state has had since Allred and those dumb bastards, dumb . . . ! Sissy has done more for Chicanos than any of those guys."[42] Once Farenthold lost the primary, the "liberal" Democrats voted for the conservative party candidate who had opposed them on every key issue of the 1972 campaign![43]

The 1974 Election

The election was unusually close in 1972, and Muniz's presence in the three-man race almost led to an unheard-of Republican victory.

A devastating defeat. In view of their surprise showing 1972, Raza Unida leaders were convinced that with more experience and organization they would surely be in a position to determine the outcome of the 1974 gubernatorial race if not actually win it. In fact, however, in terms of their percent of the vote they did no better in 1974 than they had in 1972. Given that the Democrats in Texas benefited from the Watergate backlash as well as from a more unified effort, the role Raza Unida played in 1972 was far less significant than it had been two years earlier. The defeat devastated Raza Unida. "Perhaps an obituary on Raza Unida is premature, but it is not too much to suggest that Raza Unida has no future as a statewide party, or for that matter, as a dominant political force outside a few strongholds in South Texas."[44]

Positive side of the 1974 election. Nonetheless, there were positive developments in 1974. Most importantly, Muniz did far better in heavily Chicano precincts than he did statewide. In Bexar County (San Antonio) he received 14.3 percent of the vote, and in nine Bexar precincts with 90 percent plus Chicano population, he actually outpolled Briscoe. In all precincts with more than 90 percent Chicanos Muniz trailed Briscoe by only 1.8 percent. That Muniz won his support from former Democratic voters is suggested by the fact that in 1972 McGovern had received 66 percent support in these areas in what was an off year for Democrats in the barrio.[45] Muniz did comparably well in other Chicano districts across the state. In Corpus Christi, for example, he received 23 percent of the vote; he enjoyed similar support in El Paso's Chicano precincts.[46]

The 1974 election also can be interpreted as a measure of the party's real strength. In 1972, the election was confused by division within the Democratic party and the presidential campaign. Many observers argued that Raza Unida's support was little more than a protest vote. In 1974, however, the results clearly must be interpreted as hard-core Raza Unida supporters.

Lessons of Raza Unida in Texas

The results of the statewide foray suggest a great deal about the wisdom of using such a strategy elsewhere. Clearly, the effort failed, but in failure it established a measure of its own strength.

Support from the oppressed. The fact that party votes came from those pockets of the Chicano community that are the most oppressed —the poorest barrios in San Antonio, Corpus Christi, and El Paso— reinforces the explanation we have offered for the Crystal City takeover. Chicanos in these areas recognize the depth of their poverty and exploitation, have a strong common sense of identity, are willing to attempt to change their situation, and, because they are so isolated and in such intimate contact with each other, believe they have the numbers to win.

Chicanos outside these pockets do not see themselves as completely oppressed and are not as isolated. Consequently, they do not see the need for overturning the system, and they are not convinced that Raza Unida candidates will win anyway. They are more nervous about participating in such activities because in their environment they are much more susceptible to Anglo reprisals, or they have some hope for improvement, and they are unwilling to waste their votes.

Potential power of Raza Unida. Even with only 6 percent of the vote, Raza Unida has established itself as a potential force in state elections. The Republican party in 1972 recognized this and seems to have directly or indirectly funded Raza Unida activities in the hopes that Raza Unida would either convince its constituency to vote Republican or not vote at all.[47] Since the Raza Unida voters are traditionally Democratic supporters, either change would benefit the Republicans. Raza Unida's statewide potential as a power broker can only be realized in a close election, however.[48] Thus in 1972 the party played a much greater role than it did in 1974, when the Democratic candidate for governor ran away with the election.

Implications for local success. As for change strategies, Raza Unida in Texas offers two examples. Clearly, at the local level Raza Unida can be a success, given certain structural conditions. If there is an overwhelmingly large Chicano population and if there are policies and individuals that are recognized as obvious enemies, a Chicano takeover can be achieved. Once achieved, such a takeover leads to immediate far-reaching changes that greatly benefit the Chicano community. The example of Crystal City makes it likely that takeovers in similar communities will be accomplished with relative ease. The Parlier City experience attests to this.

Theoretical meaning. From a theoretical perspective, the meaning of such takeovers is unclear. In one sense, Chicanos in Crystal City have decolonized themselves. They are in complete control of their community. Yet they could not have instituted their programs without federal financing, and at this writing the political and economic life of Crystal City is functioning very much within the accepted national norms. In other words, Gutiérrez achieved his takeover by using national political norms to escape from the practices common to South Texas, "the predemocratic zone of the United States."[49] Gutiérrez himself admits that the city might still be viewed as in internal colony with respect to its immersion in the national political system.[50] On the other hand, he defies anyone to suggest that the changes in Crystal City are insignificant.

Fundamental economic problems. Perhaps the dilemma rests on the fact that the initial changes were those easiest to effect. Replacing white officials with brown officials is a simple and traditional matter of vote getting. Elitist theorists would contend that the more fundamental problems concern the restructuring of the community's economic life, and that has not been achieved. José Angel saw his efforts as "socialistic in a small sense," and his trip to Cuba in 1975 reinforced his conviction that "capitalism has little to offer the masses of people." His plans to alter the city's economic structure include such possibilities as collective farms and the takeover of lands and feed lots currently owned by the King Ranch and other Anglo concerns. Unless he is able to realize these ends, he will not have achieved the liberation he seeks. But even without such total success, the Crystal City example stands as a change model which holds great promise to many small Chicano communities across the Southwest.

Potential for statewide efforts. The statewide effort illustrates the potential that Chicanos have to function as a meaningful pressure group. Although it lacks the resources to win statewide elections, Raza Unida clearly has the potential to mobilize significant numbers of Chicano voters into a unified voting block. Thus it can force the traditional parties to consider and respond to Chicano demands. In other words, through Raza Unida Chicanos may develop the resources to deal successfully in conventional politics on a statewide basis. Political parties are officially sanctioned by the state; access to the media usually follows.

The fact that more Chicanos do not support Raza Unida might suggest that some Chicanos have been so thoroughly colonized that they are unable to see Raza Unida as the source of their liberation, and that others see the system as sufficiently open and thus have no need for it. In either case, the Texas Raza Unida experience is not comforting to organizers in other states. Even if they are useless for winning state elections, however, such efforts probably must continue in order for local organizers to remain in contact with each other and provide one another with the logistical and moral support they need to wage their specific battles.

Change Strategy in San Antonio

While Gutiérrez engineered the Crystal City triumph, other members of MAYO/MAUC continued in their efforts to organize San Antonio. Their experience offers another example of a change strategy which could greatly benefit other communities. Undoubtedly, similar activities are already in existence elsewhere, but we use the San Antonio example because of its intimate linkage to the development of Raza Unida, because of the success these efforts have attained, and because it is the example with which the authors are most familiar.

Characteristics of the San Antonio Efforts

What is most impressive about mobilization efforts in San Antonio is that they include distinct types of organizations dealing with the entire range of Chicano concerns, and the efforts are directed at economic, educational, and political institutions. Although the organizations are concerned only with the problems confronting the Chicano community, some of the key individuals within these organizations are Anglos. Furthermore, even though these organizations have an almost exclusively Chicano constituency, they attempt to mobilize their membership without explicitly appealing to the separatist overtones often implicit in *Chicanismo*. Instead, they use the bond of ethnicity to bring people together so as to have the necessary base to participate in political and economic negotiations. The principal organizations involved in this effort are the Mexican American Unity Council (MAUC), the Southwest Voter Registration and Education Project, the Mexican American Legal Defense Fund (MALDF), Community Organized for Public Services (COPS), and the local unions, which are overwhelmingly Chicano in membership.

Except for the Chicano unions and MALDF, these organizations had their beginning in the MAUC/MAYO activities of the late 1960s. MAUC, in fact, is a modified form of the MAYO/MAUC coalition established in 1967. Willie Velasquez, Juan Patlan, and Ernie Cortez were among the initial MAYO/MAUC core, and today Velasquez heads the Southwest Voter Education Project, Patlan is chairman of MAUC, and Cortez is a major figure with COPS. They as well as the MALDF and union leaders see themselves as working toward the same goals as Gutiérrez; that is, toward creating conditions which will allow Chicanos the right of self-determination. "I like to think we still stand where we did at the beginning. I like to think we have been true to the movement." Although Patlan made this statement in reference to MAUC, it could just have easily been made by any of the other activists in reference to their own organization.

The Mexican American Unity Council

Even though these organizations share a general goal and work closely together whenever necessary, each also has a specific objective. MAUC is primarily a community development agency.

Health care, housing, and careers. Its programs include a health component which provides counseling, preschool medical care and assistance, and immunization. Another major component is its Neighborhood Housing Services program. This involves the building of rent-subsidized apartments and low-cost housing to replace less attractive conventional public housing projects. One of the objectives of this program is to offer Chicano families an opportunity to remain in the barrio. Prior to this program, families wanting to move into better houses simply had to move out of the area. With the MAUC program, this outward trend has been slowed and the barrio reinvigorated.

MAUC is also working on acquiring federal grants to guarantee loans for home improvement. City officials initially indicated they would be willing to support such efforts if only they had the funds. MAUC leaders then pointed out how the funds could be acquired, and so the city is now likely to acquire these funds. MAUC also sponsored a "New Careers" program. Participants working with government agencies were given ten hours per week to attend classes to improve their skills or acquire new ones. The program also paid for tuition and books. Unfortunately, the funding for this program has been cut off.

Business development. Perhaps the most successful activity under MAUC's control is the business development effort. This effort is designed to establish profit-making companies which will generate funds for other MAUC activities. The most successful of these is the McDonald's franchise that MAUC controls. Initially, McDonald's agreed to give MAUC control of one franchise with the opportunity to expand if the initial effort were successful. The initial franchise proved extremely successful, but McDonald's apparently bent to political pressures and refused to grant a second franchise. After extended negotiations, MAUC was able to make McDonald's respect the original agreement, and today there are two "Chicano McDonald's" in San Antonio.

The business development effort has been so successful that MAUC has received an additional grant of $769,000 to aid neighborhood business. Unfortunately, few Chicano businesses meet the eligibility guidelines, which state that only companies with ten or more employees and a gross income over $300,000 may apply for these funds.

MAUC's political role. Even though MAUC is primarily concerned with economic development, it plays an important role in the politics of the Chicano community. As a MAUC official stated, "There is no doubt we are political. There is no fooling anybody that we are very close to the liberal politicians. Some Chicano leaders see us as a threat. Others see us as *vendidos.*"

MAUC's political importance is suggested by Henry B. González's opposition to it. Congressman González not only led the fight to cut off MAUC's funds in 1969, but he undercut their activities for several years afterwards to prevent their resurgence. MAUC was on the verge of collapse until Patlan was finally able to convince the congressman that MAUC was not trying to compete with him for leadership of the Chicano community but was instead working toward his same goals. With this, "Henry B." relented and allowed MAUC to reactivate. Even today, however, the tension between González and MAUC continues. The reasons for this are unclear, but several activists suggest that González resists any activity that might challenge his authority. "He's simply not a team man."[51]

Community Organized for Public Services

COPS is the most explicitly political of these organizations. Like MAUC, COPS has organized around common problems and self-interest rather than on the basis of *Chicanismo*. The organization thus deals with problems common to Chicanos, but on a neighborhood basis, avoiding ethnic appeals. COPS is action-oriented and attacks specific problems affecting the neighborhoods such as inadequate public services, insufficient policy protection, poor drainage, and poor traffic control. Recently COPS has confronted city officials on broader questions, such as the need for utility rate hikes. Overall, COPS is extremely well organized and is having a significant impact.

In the barrio it trains community members to deal with public officials; in the city at large it makes city officials realize that they will be held accountable to the Chicano community.[52]

The Mexican American Legal Defense Fund

The MALDF staff in San Antonio also contributes greatly to Chicano political life. A national organization, MALDF was funded by the Ford Foundation in the hopes of creating a Chicano version of the NAACP Legal Defense Fund. LULAC leaders apparently were instrumental in initiating this program. MALDF's efforts in San Antonio have greatly aided the efforts of other Chicano organizations. They have been very active in educational issues, particularly those involving de facto segregation and bilingual education.

MALDF has also been at the center of the effort to protect Chicano voting rights. MALDF attorneys represented the Chicano community in its suit against the constitutionality of multimember districts.[53] When the court ruled in favor of MALDF complaint, Chicanos immediately began to win office in areas where they had seldom if ever won before. MALDF is currently trying to have the courts apply this principle to school boards and other political bodies that continue to employ multimember or at-large elections to determine their membership. The MALDF staff, led by George Korbel and utilizing the extensive research conducted by Charles Cotrell, was also instrumental in having the provisions of the 1965 Voting Rights Act extended to Texas in 1975. This inclusion benefited San Antonio activists as well as Raza Unida organizers, but for reasons that are as yet unclear, Congressman González opposed extending the bill to Texas.

MALDF has also concerned itself with discrimination in employment. Of primary concern are those practices that appear neutral but actually discriminate against Chicanos. This includes unreasonable educational requirements that are unrelated to skills needed for job performance, prohibitions against the use of Spanish on the job, and unreasonable height and weight requirements.

The Southwest Voter Education Project

This organization works closely with MALDF. The project's specific objective is to register Chicanos to vote throughout the Southwest. It is modeled after the Voter Education Project of the 1960s which played so central a role in black registration drives during the height of the civil rights movement. Despite its obvious need, this project has had a difficult time getting started. The Internal Revenue Service for several years delayed ruling on the tax-exempt status of the project, and there are those who believe this is the result of Congressman González's interference.

The project is designed to work with any existing Chicano organizations or any community groups that submit a proposal demonstrating a plan to register Chicano voters. Its funds must be used for registration and voter education programs, not to fund politicians either directly or indirectly. As of 1975, the program was struggling along on a $52,000 grant. With the extension of the Voting Rights Act to Chicano areas in the Southwest, it is likely that the project will receive additional funds and thus be in a position to implement its ten-year plan. This plan includes voter registration and education projects throughout the Southwest and in western states which have relatively large Chicano populations.

San Antonio Unions

The final component of the combined San Antonio effort is the Chicano-dominated unions. Their role in San Antonio politics is illustrated by the experiences of the local garment worker's union.

The garment workers' strike. Prior to the Farah strike which began in the late 1960s, the Chicano garment workers were relatively apolitical and almost totally unconscious of the Chicano movement. The Farah strike, however, became a national issue and put them into the spotlight. Chicano politicians throughout the city, with the notable exception of Henry B. González, endorsed the strike, and these events quickly sharpened the political consciousness of the Chicano worker. They began working in electoral campaigns as they had never done before.

The impact of the politicization seems permanent to the labor leadership. One leader said, "They'll never go back, they can't go back to their non-involvement." The strike affected the entire city, and the Chicano community joined together to wage their battle. Thus, the newly developed politicization of the garment workers stimulated other unions and the community in general, and their triumph in 1974 over the Farah Corporation has further convinced them that collectively the community has the power to influence both public and private decisions.[54]

The unions and Raza Unida. Significantly, the unions do not work with Raza Unida. Union leaders describe themselves as pragmatic and consider Raza Unida leaders to be out of touch with reality. In 1974, the unions supported a Raza Unida candidate for the state legislature not because he was Raza Unida but because he was pragmatic in his approach to community problems. The unions, however, did not endorse Muniz for governor in 1974 for two reasons. First, at the state level the AFL-CIO endorsed the Democrats, and the local leadership decided not to go against this decision even though they could have. More importantly, according to a key union leader, "Raza Unida did not address labor problems. Ramsey was with us during the 1972 election and then left us alone later. This seemed like rhetorical support to us."

Bonds Among San Antonio Organizations

In combination, these Chicano organizations have developed a formidable political presence. There is regular communication among the groups, and the leadership is in such intimate contact that it often seems to overlap. San Antonio officials are now conscious of this political force and have been forced into dealing with it. Where once Chicano demands were shelved or shuffled from office to office, now they are at least dealt with if not met.

Several bonds make this cooperative effort possible. First, the constituency is almost completely Chicano. The mobilization efforts have focused around economic issues and not ethnic issues, however. Thus the battle of the "name" has not been fought. To the members and the leadership the problem of self-identification is irrelevant. They are certain and confident of their ethnicity and, unlike many Chicanos in California, Denver and elsewhere, do not feel the need to mobilize around that issue. The leadership, many of whom call themselves Chicano, know that the label is divisive. "The strikers were surprised to hear about the Chicano issue. The word is still offensive. So we switched to 'nosotros los trabajadores.' ('we the workers')."

This pragmatic approach does not mean to suggest that the leadership and many of the members do not feel themselves a major part of the Chicano movement. The following statement by Juan Patlan reflects the views expressed by leaders in other organizations. "José Ángel established a political party that had to be approved by the state. He decided that San Antonio was unmanageable while Crystal City was manageable. He's done a fantastic job, but so have we. He wants to isolate

San Antonio by taking over cities all around us. We want to make changes here."

Lessons from the San Antonio Experience

This model would then seem to hold several lessons for other Chicano communities. First, as Deluvina Hernandez stated, the Chicano movement manifests itself and achieves it objectives in a variety of ways.

Reasons for success. The leaders of the Chicano organizations in San Antonio are at the personal level defiantly Chicano, but they seem more pragmatic than ideological—they are more concerned with immediate short-range objectives than long-term goals. There is no denying that their efforts have helped meet some of the demands of the barrio. It is also clear that to engage successfully in this type of politics you must above all know where power resides. For a time, the MAUC leadership refused to deal with Congressman Gonzalez, and he thwarted them. It was only when they neutralized him that they were able to make any headway. Similarly, the leadership knew that through the mobilization of a massive voting bloc they could make heretofore callous officials come to the bargaining table.

Importance of immediate improvements. This approach also made clear that low-level, issue-specific, incremental victories are important to the community. However trivial improvements such as sidewalks, paved streets, and parks are to the ideological revolutionary, to many Chicanos these are significant indeed. By helping Chicanos satisfy these demands, these organizations have won the confidence and trust of the people. Now they can use this trust to attack the more significant problems of institutional racism which are at the roots of the systematic denial of public services to Chicano neighborhoods.[55]

From a revolutionary perspective, it is easy to find fault with these successes. In addition to being trivial, they may help depoliticize the community by convincing potential revolutionary masses that the system is responsive. Furthermore, such a gradual approach might never allow the community to attack the fundamental structure oppressing the Chicano population—the capitalistic structure.

The only response that can be made to these indictments is that the people involved most intimately with these problems, the Chicanos in the barrio, want an immediate improvement in their situation. To deny the significance of these real although modest improvements is to deny the legitimacy of the demands coming from the community itself. The impact that these incremental achievements have made on the San Antonio community is as real and obvious as the impact of those made in Crystal City. Again, whether such changes in fact will lead to the liberation of Chicanos can not yet be determined. They do not, however, necessarily prevent liberation.

Importance of cooperation. The approach and success of these organizations would seem to have great meaning for many other Chicano communities. Above all, neither Crystal City nor San Antonio have exclusive claims to articulate, sophisticated, and intelligent leadership. Anyone familiar with Chicano communities across the Southwest knows that comparable leaders are making themselves known throughout the area. What is unusual is the willingness of the Texas groups to cooperate so intimately and effectively.

The San Antonio example illustrates the significance of such cooperation, and it should encourage other communities to copy this strategy. While Crystal City may serve as an example to only a few rural areas, San Antonio stands as a model for every major city in the Southwest. Of course the degree of success that might be achieved in other cities will be at least partially influenced by the size of the local Chicano population. But the lesson of San Antonio is clear: some success can be achieved if only the existing resources are wisely utilized.

Chapter 10
Notes

1. Tony Castro, "La Raza Convenes," *Texas Observer*, 22 September 1972, p. 4.
2. Deluvina Hernandez, "La Raza Satellite System," *Aztlan* 1 (Spring, 1970): 13-36.
3. Interview at Colorado College, May 14, 1975.
4. Richard Santillan, *La Raza Unida* (Los Angeles: Tlaquilo Publications, 1973), pp. 12-19.
5. Armando Rendon, *Chicano Manifesto* (New York: Collier, 1971), p. 226.
6. Matt S. Meier and Feliciano Rivera, *The Chicanos* (New York: Hill and Wang, 1972), p. 277.

7. Santillan, *La Raza Unida*, p. 53.

8. Ibid., p. 54.

9. Raza Unida Party Platform, Tucson, undated.

10. Partido de la Raza Unida, 1972 Platform, Colorado.

11. Texas Raza Unida Party, "A Political Action Program for the 70's," undated, p. 20.

12. Santillan, *La Raza Unida*, p. 53; *Raza Unida* Platform, Tucson.

13. See chapter 4 for a discussion of the key issues.

14. Santillan, *La Raza Unida*, pp. 51-54.

15. Alberto Juarez, "The Emergence of El Partido de la Raza Unida: California's New Chicano Party," in *La Causa Politica*, ed. F. Chris Garcia (Notre Dame: University of Notre Dame Press, 1974), p. 311.

16. Ibid., pp. 312-313.

17. Ibid., p. 314.

18. F. Chris Garcia and Robert Wrinkle, "Urban Politics in a State of Varying Political Cultures," in *Politics in the Urban Southwest*, ed. Robert Wrinkle (Division of Government Research Publication no. 81, University of New Mexico, 1971).

19. For a discussion of different types of Chicano organizations see George Rivera, Jr., "Nosotros Venceremos: Chicano Consciousness and Change Strategies," *Journal of Applied Behavioral Science,* 8, no. 1 (Jan.-Feb., 1972) 56-71.

20. Corky Gonzáles is nonetheless a controversial figure. See Rudolph O. de la Garza and John Womack, Jr., "An Exchange on the Chicanos," *The New York Review of Books*, 19 April 1973, pp. 41-42.

21. Alfredo Cuellar, "Perspectives on Politics: Part I," in *La Causa*, ed. Garcia, pp. 46-47, indicates that the Chicano movement in California might also have started with the activities of college students.

22. The material presented in the remainder of this chapter is from interviews conducted with Chicano leaders in San Antonio in November-December 1974, and during several visits to San Antonio through September, 1975. The data on Crystal City is from interviews conducted in December 1974. See Tony Castro, *Chicano Power* (New York: Saturday Review Press, 1974), pp. 148-162.

23. John Shockley, *Chicano Revolt in a Texas Town* (Notre Dame: University of Notre Dame Press, 1974), is correct when he cites MAYO as the origin

of the Crystal City takeover, but he may not have grasped the broader implications and wider impact of MAYO's activities and leadership development.

24. Henry B. Gonzalez, "The Hate Issue," reprinted in Garcia, *Chicano Politics,* pp. 102-107.

25. Shockley, *Chicano Revolt.*

26. As quoted in John R. Fry, "Election Night in Crystal City," *Christianity and Crisis* 32, no. 20 (November 27, 1972): 254. See also Castro, *Chicano Power*, pp. 148-164.

27. Shockley, *Chicano Revolt*, indicates these are several of the factors that make the Crystal City experience unique and not replicable elsewhere.

28. Joe R. Reagin and Harlan Hahn, *Ghetto Revolts* (New York: MacMillan, 1973), posit that similar attitudes among the black community were a major factor in the riots of the 1960s.

29. Shockley, *Chicano Revolt*; *Wall Street Journal*, 5 September 1975, p. 19; *Texas Observer*, 5 July 1974; Castro, *Chicano Power.*

30. Personal interview, December 1974.

31. Robert Aguallo, Jr., and Adaljiza Sosa Riddell, "Local Politics, Local Elites and Political Change: The Case of Parlier, California," paper presented at the Western Political Science Association meeting, March 1975.

32. Shockley, *Chicano Revolt*, pp. 224-226.

33. Antonio Camejo, "A Report from Aztlan," in *La Causa*, ed. Garcia, p. 234. See also Rivera, "Nosotros Venceremos," for a description of the conditions which lead to such changes.

34. *Wall Street Journal*, 5 September 1975, p. 19.

35. *Texas Observer*, 7 July 1974.

36. *Texas Observer* 25 August 1972. As might be expected of a decolonizing movement, Ramsey Muniz, who was one of the first leaders, is among the most acculturated of Raza Unida activists.

37. *Texas Observer*, 25 August 1972.

38. Jose A. Ramirez, "Three Political Platforms: An Evaluation," unpublished manuscript, 1973.

39. Castro, "La Raza Convenes," p. 4.

40. *Texas Observer*, 25 August 1972.

41. Castro, "La Raza Convenes," p. 5. Farenthold was the liberal challenger for the Democratic nomination for governor in the 1972 and 1974 Texas

elections. Her candidacy was particularly hopeful in 1972 as a result of widespread scandals that shook the Democratic party in 1971-72.

42. *Texas Observer*, 25 August 1972.

43. The unwillingness of Texas liberal and moderate Democrats to support Muniz is surely the result of the maintenance of traditional voting patterns (that is allegiance to the Democratic party), the distrust of Muñiz because of his inexperience and an unarticulated racism. There is no way to determine how much each of these factors contributed to the failure of white communities to support Muñiz.

44. Tony Castro, *Texas Observer*, 29 November 1974.

45. Rolando Cortes and Andrew Hernandez, Jr., "Raza Unida: A Study of Raza Unida Party Strength in Bexar County and South Texas," unpublished, undated manuscript.

46. *Texas Observer*, 29 November 1974.

47. Ibid., 14 December 1973.

48. Armando G. Gutierrez, "Institutional Completeness and La Raza Unida Party," in *Chicanos and Native Americans*, ed. Rudolph O. de la Garza, A. Anthony Kruszewski, and Tomas A. Arciniega (New York: Prentice-Hall, 1973), pp. 113-123.

49. Fry, "Election in Crystal City," p. 256.

50. Personal interview, December 1974.

51. Shockley, *Chicano Revolt*, pp. 124-125, further documents Congressman Gonzalez's personalistic style.

52. We would like to thank COPS for allowing us to observe some of their activities from within. In respect of their request, we have limited our description of the organization, membership, and tactics to that information which is available in the public press.

53. See Charles L. Cotrell, "The Effects of At-Large Elections on the Political Access and Voting Strength of Mexican Americans and Blacks in Texas," a paper presented at the Rocky Mountain Social Science Convention, April 1975.

54. The strikers "triumphed" in that the Farah Corporation came to terms with the strikers in El Paso. Prior to this agreement, however, Farah closed its plant in San Antonio. Despite the closing, the Farah strikers claim victory.

55. Charles L. Cotrell, "Municipal Services Equalization and Internal Colonialism in San Antonio, Texas: Explorations in Chinatown," a paper presented at the Rocky Mountain Social Science Convention, April 1975.

Analyses, Conclusions, and Prospects

The concluding chapter on the Chicanos' political experience in the United States cannot yet be written. The most recent and forceful Chicano political movement is only a decade old. Progress during this period has been significant, if not substantial, particularly when compared to the minor influence exercised by Chicanos since 1848.

Complexity of Chicano Politics

Any tentative conclusions or projections must take into account a multitude of factors, for the situation is extremely complex. To understand Chicano politics one must attempt to comprehend the historical development of the Chicano as well as analyze the specific contemporary conditions affecting Chicanos. Moreover, the Chicano people are themselves changing. Forces of urbanization, education, technology, increased acculturation to core-culture America, continued immigration from Mexico, and a heightened political consciousness are just a few of the causes of change. And the changes in the American society in which Chicano politics take place are at least as complicated, perhaps even incapable of being really understood. Economic, social, cultural, and technological developments are occurring at such a rapid rate that even core-culture Americans are disoriented and thrown into "future shock."

This is the unstable environment in which the United States political system operates. To further worsen the situation, the politics and government of the United States are probably the most complicated and difficult to understand of any modern political system. Thus, the best we can hope to do in this limited space is to review and summarize the past and current status of Chicanos in American politics, try to suggest the most appropriate interpretation—pluralist, elite, or internal colonial—of American politics, relate these interpretations to contemporary trends, and venture some analyses and projections as to the future relationship of the Chicano people and the American political system.

Changes in Chicano Politics, 1966-1976

We have seen that there has been a tremendous quantitative and qualitative change in the political activity of Chicanos in the United States over the past ten years. This quickening of the pace has been termed the Chicano Movement. Althought the Movement is in many was a continuation of past political activities, it is also in many ways a more forceful, influential, and innovative mode of activity. The Movement has brought the Chicanos' situation before the core culture to the extent that the power structures in the United States have had no choice but to deal with the Chicano. At the same time there has been a very noticeable increase in the awareness among Chicanos that political action is necessary to overcome the problems common to them throughout the United States.

The term "Chicano" itself tells us a great deal about what has happened the last few years. "Chicano" is now commonly used by the mass media in this country and is increasingly a term of common recognition throughout the Mexican and Spanish-American peoples of this nation. It is obvious that something of importance in the relationship of Chicanos to American politics has occurred since the mid-1960s. In spite of the denials of those favoring the internal colonial model, the Chicano has made real progress in many substantive areas.

All the traditional indicators of well-being in this country indicate that more Chicanos today are enjoying a better life. The gap in income between Chicanos and Anglos has closed somewhat; Chicanos are becoming more middle class, although the income gap is still wide and deep. More Chicanos are attending school, including colleges and universities, than ever before, and educational institutions are modifying their programs and curriculum to better serve Chicano children. Chicanos are also staying in school longer.

Lest the pluralists and other defenders of the status quo claim that the system is open and just after all, it should be pointed out that these gains made by Chicanos are only incremental and have occurred through determined, persevering, and sometimes extraordinary efforts by the Chicano people. And their efforts have usually been met by a great deal of resistance. The gains may indeed be temporary, and the inequalities between the Mexican-American and Anglo-American people are still substantial. It is not certain how really important these changes are to the overall status of the Chicano in the American system.

Pluralist Interpretation of Changes

The big question, of course, is: "Has the Chicano movement fundamentally altered the basic distribution of power in the American system?" That is, are Chicanos now a significant element in the power configuration of the United States? The pluralists and defenders of the system would probably say, "Yes, a start has been made and continued efforts will bring the Chicano people rewards corresponding to their efforts. These economic, educational, and political gains made by Chicanos can be the basis for further advances. After all, along with the indicators of mass improvement, there is the fact that individual Chicanos have entered more important decision-making positions in the American system. There are now Chicano bank presidents, Chicanos on corporation boards of directors, and more Chicano representatives in state legislatures. Indeed even two of the five Southwestern states' governors are Chicanos. These advances will lay the base for further improvements by adding to the resources that the Chicano people can muster in their political activities."

This defense makes some sense, particularly when applied at the local and state levels. The successes in Crystal City and Parlier, California, in the agricultural fields and in state and local governments of the Southwest, strengthen the arguments of the pluralists. However, these localized victories, while bringing real gains to the people in those areas, are not very secure, because local and state governments are so dependent upon national economic and political institutions. Thus victories by Chicanos at this level are in at least one sense rather shallowly rooted. The pluralists may indeed be correct when their arguments are applied to state and local governmental levels, but their analysis is much less convincing when one expands the view to the national scene.

Elitist Interpetation of Changes

At the national level the elite analysis of American politics makes at least as much sense as that of pluralists. Those powerful economic and political interests that elite theorists see as controlling this country have remained basically unaffected by the Chicano movement.

Exclusion of Chicanos from National Government

Chicanos have not secured any major decision-making positions in the executive branch of the United States government. The few gains they made in the early 1970s have almost all been wiped out.[1] Only those who were entirely coopted have survived, and because of their change in values, they are no longer of much help to the rest of the Chicano people. Chicanos are not found in the high positions of powerful national economic institutions such as major banks, insurance companies, petroleum producers, steel industries, the mass transportation and communication industries, and other major corporations in America. The military establishment at the highest levels does not include people of Mexican/Spanish ancestry. It is only the middle or lower levels of decision making in the United States that are open to advances by Chicanos. Although it is true that these advances have some payoffs, it is also true that achieving these positions tends to lessen the pressures to advance any further and to challenge the real centers of power in the United States.

Lack of Advancement Among Masses

The masses of Chicano people are not much better off than they were. While more of them may be making more money than in the past, this is generally true of the rest of society. Also, the advances in standard of living are not great—only enough to forestall any mass demands for a radical redistribution of wealth in the country. Chicanos are still the last hired and the first to be fired. Most Chicanos still work for other people—they do not own the means of production and distribution of goods. Even though more brown faces may be seen in the media, they do not control the means of mass communication so important to influencing public opinion in our society. In fact economic hard times such as a recession show that many Chicano advances are essentially minor, temporary, and dependent on an expanding economic pie and the willingness of the power structures to grant economic and political concessions to the Chicano. The economic, political, and educational concessions or tokens that Chicanos have gained demonstrate only that the elite power structure will allow groups to improve their lots as long as the powerholders themselves are not threatened.

Thus, minor gains in material goods and token positions attained by coopted leaders do not signify a major redistribution of power in this country or even the beginnings of such a reformation. These are only low- and middle-level occurrences which in no way change the fact that the power structure in the United States is biased and closed to the advances of the Chicano people as well as to others.

The pluralists then can take some comfort from the small amount of perhaps superficial change that has occurred due to Chicano politics. Their generally optimistic bias sees these small advances as meaning greater changes somewhere off in the future. The elitists, on the other hand, will dismiss these changes as inconsequential in the long run and perhaps even preventing major changes in the future. Nevertheless, as descriptive or analytical models, the pluralist ideas seem to have at least face validity when applied to local and, to a lesser extent, state political systems. At the national level that closed and pessimistic model of the elitists seems to offer at least as good an explanation of what has happened and what in all likelihood will not happen.

Internal Colonialist Interpretation of Changes

Those who favor the internal colonial model are probably forced to admit that their model can not adequately account for the successes of the Chicano political movement over the past several years. Indeed their analysis would seem to serve much better as a dramatic and fairly accurate description of the *historical* reasons for the Chicanos' status. The notion of physical conquest of the Chicano people and their lands and the consequent management of their lives by the victors, of the importance of racism as a barrier to Chicano hopes, of the record of systematic attempts to belittle cultures different from the Anglo core culture is convincing and historically compelling.

Inability to Account for Advances

However, it fails to account for the advances made by the Chicano people over the past several years. Chicanos are controlling their affairs to a greater extent than ever before. The political, educational, and communications institutions of our society have made significant changes in their programs in response to the demands of Chicanos that their culture and people be presented in a less insulting manner

—that their culture be promoted rather than negatively stereotyped. As a matter of fact, there seems to be a renewed interest on the part of many nonracial minority people in the United States in preserving and promoting their ethnic and cultural heritage.[2]

Various affirmative action programs have been instituted, and while far from being the successes that some of their defenders would claim, such programs have resulted in increased opportunities to many Chicano people. The outright brutality by police and other law enforcement agencies is pretty much a thing of the past. Law enforcement agencies have set up community relations boards, made efforts to recruit minority members, and initiated other programs to get together with Chicano community members. Government-sponsored agencies such as the U.S. Commission on Civil Rights have made public some serious criticisms about law enforcement agencies of the government. And the media report and publicize these injustices.

Lack of Realistic Solution

Another shortcoming of the internal colonial model is that it offers very little direction to Chicanos seeking "liberation." What kind of political strategies and tactics follow from the acceptance of the internal colonial model? Pluralist strategies such as elections, pressure group activity, and political parties are seen as ineffective or even harmful to the cause. Chicanos who become decision makers are seen as necessarily *vendidos* (sellouts) and of no use to the Chicano masses. It would seem that the *only* real political solution would be for Chicanos to become entirely separate from the rest of American society in their economic, educational, social, and political affairs. Such a complete separation seems so unlikely, in the bright light of reality, that this goal can only be dismissed as either foolhardy or based on many inaccurate assumptions. So the internal colonial model is very helpful in explaining the history of the Chicano people and even some of their current conditions. It has been useful as a teaching model, an easily grasped and forcefully presented idea. It has been politically exciting as a mobilizing idea. But it does not seem to be of much use as an accurate descriptive of analytical model of modern-day conditions, or as a guide to future directions for the Chicano movement.[3]

Current Status of the Movement

Currently the Chicano political movement is in a stage of institutionalization. The dramatic and heated politics of the early 1970s are rarely in evidence. Instead many of the gains are being consolidated. It is to be hoped that some of these have been institutionalized to the extent that advances will continue to be made in a semi-automatic process.

Uncertain Nature of Gains

Unfortunately, some of the advances will most certainly be lost. For instance, Chicano studies programs on the nation's campuses are increasingly subject to neglect if not attack. The whole idea of affirmative action (government intervention to remedy past injustice to disadvantaged groups) has produced a massive backlash, particularly among those middle- and lower-middle-class whites who have just barely secured their own status in American society. In many cases the movement for women's liberation overshadows the continuing needs of ethnic minorities.

The uncertainties of the United States economy in the mid-1970s has also chipped away at the economic gains of the earlier years. Chicanos are once again being unemployed at a very high rate. Many of the governmental programs which boosted the efforts of Chicanos in the late 1960s and early 1970s have now been sacrificed on the altar of governmental austerity programs (while, of course, other governmental expenditures continue to increase at their habitual pace).

It is doubtful that the slight gains made by Chicanos have provided the kind of resource base sufficient for them to compete on an equal footing in any large arena of pluralistic politics. Nor has such a radical consciousness been aroused among enough people that Chicanos are ready or willing to challenge any major stronghold of elitist power in the United States. In many ways, Chicanos are still the victims of their internal colonial past.

Significance of Progress

But the material advances and the psychological reinforcement brought about by the long history of Chicano political struggles in the United States, and more particularly by the political activities during the Movement era, are far from inconsequential. Progress, however slight, has been made, and the opportunities for further progress have been increased. The social and political consciousness of a major segment of the American population has been restructured—Chicanos are no longer willing to contentedly accept the injustices and abuses of the system. Much of the rest of American society recognizes that this change has occurred. Some are aware of it and are slightly frightened; some pretend that it does not exist and hope that if ignored, it will go away.

Conclusion

Many Americans believe that the Chicano movement has added a new and valuable element to the societal and political mix that constitutes this country's way of life. The Chicano culture is seen by many Americans as offering some exciting and attractive alternatives to the dominant core culture's lifestyles. Although the effects of urbanization, education, and the mass media will tend to push the Chicano closer to the American mainstream, Chicanos will continue to be a distinctive and significant element in this country's politics. Their cultural source, their motherland, is adjacent to the United States and thousands of Mexicans still become in fact, if not by law, Mexican Americans every year. At the same time, many Chicanos are almost imperceptibly making their way into various institutions of American society. The Chicano people have a long history of endurance and perseverance, which will certainly continue into the future.

The dynamic interaction of all these forces will most assuredly result in some significant changes in the relationship of the Chicano to United States politics. The system, unable to ignore the change, will be pressured to live up to its democratic ideology of equality, justice, and brotherhood. Chicano politics, having been accelerated and invigorated by the Chicano political movement, are here to stay, and neither the Chicano people nor the United States political system will ever be the same again.

Chapter 11
Notes

1. See, for example, the newspaper articles by Tony Castro and Peggy Simpson reprinted in *La Causa Politica: A Chicano Political Reader,* ed. F. Chris Garcia (Notre Dame University Press, 1974), pp. 153-161.

2. Michael Novack, *The Rise of the Unmeltable Ethnics* (New York: Macmillan, 1971); Perry L. Weed, *The White Ethnic Movement and Ethnic Politics* (New York: Praeger Publications, 1973); Michael Wenk, S. M. Tomasi, and Geno Baroni, eds., *Pieces of a Dream: The Ethnic Worker's Crises in America* (New York: Center for Migration Studies, 1972).

3. The utility of internal colonialism has recently been reexamined in two studies which come to somewhat different conclusions. See F. A. Cervantes, "Chicano Politics as Internal Colonialism and American Pluralism: A Conceptual Paradox," paper presented at the International Studies Association Meeting, Toronto, April 1976; and Rudolph O. de la Garza and Charles Cotrell, "Chicanos and Internal Colonialism: A Reconceptualization," paper presented at the International Studies Association Meeting, Toronto, April 1976.

Glossary

Aztlan: the mythical northern kingdom of the Aztecs, now the southwestern United States.

bandido: bandit.

barrio: Mexican American neighborhood. A barrio is not necessarily a lower-class, dilapidated area.

bato loco: the Chicano equivalent of a black street dude.

carnales: brothers.

carnalismo: brotherhood. Used to suggest the shared feelings and objectives of Chicanos.

la Chicana: the woman member of the Chicano movement. In Spanish, terms such as *Chicano* and *hijos*, when used generally, refer to both sexes. *Hijos* thus may be used to identify one's sons and daughters just as *Chicanos* may refer to Chicanos and Chicanas. Chicanos is therefore not a sexist term, and *La Chicana* is used for emphasis.

Chicanismo: The label given to the Mexican American's recently articulated feeling of cultural nationalism, political activism, or ethnic pride.

doña: a title of respect and courtesy given to older ladies in Spanish-speaking society.

envidia: envy.

la familia: family. Here the reference is to the extended family which includes distant cousins, aunts, and other relatives.

gavacho: a pejorative synonym for Anglo American.

gringo: a less pejorative synonym for Anglo American.

hacienda: a large landed estate, often completely self-contained.

Hispano: A term used to identify the Spanish-speaking citizens of northern New Mexico. The term emphasizes the Spanish as opposed to Mexican or Indian ancestry of northern New Mexicans. Younger northern New Mexicans are increasingly identifying as Chicanos.

huelga: strike.

machismo: the masculine sense of pride, honor, and dignity. Contemporary usage by non-Chicanos incorrectly equates machismo with sexual prowess, brutality, and combativeness.

mestizo. a person with Spanish and Indian blood. Most Chicanos are *mestizos.*

migra. slang term for the Immigration and Nationalization Service.

Movimiento Estudiantil Chicano de Aztlan (MECHA): Chicano Student Movement of Aztlan.

pachuco: the original Chicano *bato loco.* First appeared in El Paso but became famous in Los Angeles. Characterized by a distinctive and exaggeratedly elegant clothing style and tatooed hands.

Penitentes: a secret religious brotherhood established in New Mexico during the second half of the nineteenth century.

personalismo: an attitude or behavioral style that emphasizes the individual rather than the group or an ideology.

Raza. another term, less value-laden, for Chicano or Mexican-American.

Respeto: respect.

rinches: a pejorative nickname for the Texas Rangers.

tia: aunt.

tio taco: a Chicano sellout. Equivalent to an Uncle Tom.

unidad: unity.

vendido: a sellout. Usually used against Chicanos who have assimilated or against Chicano officials who respond primarily to Anglo demands.

Index